Economics of the Madhouse

Economics of the Madhouse

Capitalism and the market today

Chris Harman

BOOKMARKS

London, Chicago and Sydney

Economics of the Madhouse – Chris Harman
First published September 1995
Reprinted February 1997
Bookmarks Publications Ltd, 265 Seven Sisters Road, London N4 2DE
Bookmarks, PO Box 16085, Chicago, Illinois, 60616, USA
Bookmarks, PO Box A338, Sydney South, NSW 2000, Australia
Copyright © Bookmarks Publications Ltd

ISBN 1 898876 03 7

Printed by BPC Wheatons Ltd, Exeter
Cover design by Ian Goodyer and Sherborne Design

Bookmarks Publications Ltd is linked to an international grouping of socialist organisations:
- **Australia:** International Socialists, PO Box A338, Sydney South NSW 2000
- **Belgium:** Socialisme International, Rue Lovinfosse 60, 4030 Grivengée,
- **Britain:** Socialist Workers Party, PO Box 82, London E3
- **Canada:** International Socialists, PO Box 339, Station E, Toronto, Ontario M6H 4E3
- **Cyprus:** Ergatiki Demokratia, PO Box 7280, Nicosia
- **Denmark:** Internationale Socialister, Postboks 642, 2200 København N,
- **France:** Socialisme International, BP 189, 75926 Paris Cedex 19
- **Greece:** Organosi Sosialisliki Epanastasi, c/o Workers Solidarity, PO Box 8161, Athens 100 10,
- **Holland:** International Socialists, PO Box 9720, 3506 GR Utrecht
- **Ireland:** Socialist Workers Party, PO Box 1648, Dublin 8
- **Norway:** Internasjonale Socialisterr, Postboks 9226 Gronland, 0134 Oslo
- **Poland:** Solidarność Socjalistyczna, PO Box 12, 01-900 Warszawa 118
- **South Africa:** Socialist Workers Organisation, PO Box 18530, Hillbrow 2038, Johannesburg
- **Spain:** Socialismo International, Apartado 563, 08080, Barcelona
- **United States:** International Socialist Organization, PO Box 16085, Chicago, Illinois 60616
- **Zimbabwe:** International Socialists, PO Box 6758, Harare

Contents

Introduction 7

1 A world gone mad 11

2 Explaining the crisis 32

3 Getting worse 45

4 Getting bigger 63

5 Things fall apart 85

6 Further reading 106

Chris Harman is a leading member of the Socialist Workers Party and is the editor of *Socialist Worker*. He is the author of numerous books, pamphlets and articles including *Explaining the Crisis, How Marxism Works, The Lost Revolution: Germany 1918-23, Class Struggles in Eastern Europe* and *The Fire Last Time: 1968 and After.*

Introduction

We are continually told that capitalism is the only economic system that can work. The reality for most of the world's five billion people today is that it is not working in our interests.

The World Health Organisation reports that the biggest killer in the world today is not coronary thrombosis or cancer, but 'deep poverty' in which a thousand million people live. Such poverty is a growing feature of life even in the industrially advanced countries, where there are more than 30 million people wholly unemployed and another 15 million in insecure temporary and part time jobs according to the latest figures from the Organisation for Economic Cooperation and Development. In the United States—the richest society in the whole of human history—32 million people were living below the poverty line in 1988 (at the height of the 1980s boom) and nearly one in five children were born into poverty. In Britain a third of children grow up in poverty.

People with jobs face greater insecurity and stress than at any time in the last half century. 'Work is the major cause of stress, according to a survey of more than 5,000 office workers in 16 countries', reports the *Financial Times*. 'More than half the respondents said stress levels had risen over the past two years'.

There is relentless pressure on the mass of people to work more and accept less pay than in the past. This is shown most vividly in the United States, where real wages have been falling for 20 years. According to the *Los Angeles Times*, The US Department of Commerce notes:

From 1973 real wages fell at an annual compound rate of 0.7 percent. This trend continues. In the three months up to June 1974, the purchasing power of US workers fell by 0.7 percent.

A study by Juliet Schor called *The Overworked American* speaks of the 'unexpected decline of leisure':

Americans now work an average of 164 hours more annually than 20 years ago. This amounts to about a month more at work per year.

In Britain, Germany and most of the rest of Western Europe real wages were rising until recently. But here too the pressure is now on. In Britain there has been an attempt at a complete public sector wage freeze. In Germany new taxes are due to cut the living standards of working class families. And in both countries Tory politicians are telling us we've had it too good for too long.

Thus German prime minister Helmut Kohl says West Germany must 'adapt to profound changes in its way of life with longer working hours', while British employment minister Michael Portillo claims, 'Europeans pay themselves too much' and have holidays that are 'too long' and working weeks that are 'too short'. Politicians tell us that we have to stop expecting to have 'jobs for life' and that we have to look at ways to cut down on the 'economic burden' of paying pensions to a growing number of old people.

This is now all part of the conventional economic wisdom preached by major governments. It is reinforced by the growing influence of what used to be ideas confined to the lunatic fringe of the right. In the US people like Charles Murray have gained a huge hearing for their contention that if growing numbers of people are living in poverty, this is the fault of welfare provision which has created an 'underclass' of feckless people unable to seize the opportunities open to them. The only answer, the 'new right' claim, is to abolish welfare provision for unmarried mothers who insist on having more children. In Britain too there is growing talk of the danger of 'welfare dependency'— talk which is beginning to be heard in the Labour Party as well as Tory circles.

If there are pools of poverty in the industrially advanced countries, there are huge seas of it in much of the rest of the world. The continents of Africa and Latin America actually got poorer in the 1970s and 1980s, with average income per head falling. While the poor have to scrimp and save to get by in Europe and the US, they starve by the millions in parts of Africa.

There is little hope either in much of the former Eastern bloc. In 1989 people were promised that the market would bring them a new 'economic miracle'. Five years later people were even worse off materially than under the old dictatorships, with living standards cut by 40 or 50 percent.

Yet not everybody is poor. The very rich are better off than ever before. In 1980 the top managers of the 300 biggest US companies had incomes 29 times larger than that of the average manufacturing worker; by 1990 their incomes were 93 times greater. While two billion people live on or below the breadline in 'third world' countries, a thin upper layer live increasingly luxurious lives. The *Financial Times* could report in February 1995 on how private banks catering for such people were flourishing: 'Rich people in Europe and the Middle East are estimated by Chase Manhattan…to have some 1,000 billion pounds in cash or liquid assets… Latin America and Asia account for a further 1,000 billion of private wealth, a figure which is growing fast.'

In the US highly paid 'experts' want an end to welfare payments to ease the burden on the rich of keeping the poor alive; in Brazil the rich pay death squads to kill teenagers who sleep in the streets.

In the midst of this poverty and squalor a hundred and one other evils have flourished. Old diseases like TB, cholera and even bubonic plague—Black Death—have reappeared. Addiction to hard drugs has spread as people see them as the only way to escape, however temporarily, from their suffering. Suicide rates have soared. Crime has grown as a minority of the poor see in it the only hope of matching the luxury lives of the rich flaunted before them by the advertising agencies. On top of all this there has been the horrific scourge of war, with the United Nations Human Development Report warning that 'persistent threats from hunger, violence and illness are the root cause of the increasing number of internal conflicts worldwide…' and noting that states, big and small, would rather spend billions on modern weapons systems than cater for people's desperate needs.

Poverty and disease, hunger and pain, hopelessness and desperation are not, of course, something new in human society. They have existed throughout most of recorded history.

But the poverty in the world today is different. For it exists alongside wealth on a scale easily sufficient to banish poverty for ever. In 1992 the total economic output of the whole world was five times what it was in 1950, according to the United Nations Human Development Report. Yet poverty, in many parts of the world is as bad today, if not worse than 45 years ago. Hunger exists alongside huge stockpiles of food—witness the European Union's food mountains—while governments in America and Europe pay farmers not to plant their land. People are told there is not enough wealth to go round while firms close factories and sack people who could be producing more wealth. The mass of people are told they cannot have jobs unless they work longer and harder for lower wages, while in every country a small minority at the top live it up as never before. In 1950 the richest fifth of the world's population took 30 percent of its incomes; today they take 60 percent. Meanwhile, the poorest fifth of humanity are left to share a mere 1.4 percent of total world output.

Few of those who support the present organisation of society expect things to get better. In many countries there are parties, like the Labour Party in Britain, that once promised to improve the condition of the poor with full employment, greater spending on welfare and a redistribution of income from the rich to the poor. Today they tell us these ideas are 'old fashioned'.

A huge conundrum confronts us which none of the established political parties can come to terms with. More wealth is being produced than ever before in history. There are inventions for increasing the output of all sorts of things, including the basic foods denied to generations of humanity. Human beings can conquer outer space and explore the depths of the oceans. They can use machines to do backbreaking toil or send information from one side of the world to the other in a fraction of a second. Yet far from the burden of securing a livelihood getting lighter it is often getting heavier. Instead of people looking forward to living more prosperous and comfortable lives, often they can only live in fear of things getting worse. Far from poverty disappearing, it grows.

CHAPTER 1

A world gone mad

1 The poverty of economics

Professional economists are meant to be able to tell us how all this has come about. Yet anyone who looks to them for illumination will be sorely disillusioned.

The dominant capitalist school of economics today is called the 'marginal' or 'neo-classical' school. This is what you will be taught if you study economics at further education colleges, in an adult education class or at university. Its proponents claim that their economics is a technical discipline, 'the human science that studies the relationship between scarce resources and the various uses which compete for these resources'.

Production takes place, they claim, according to the 'law of supply and demand'. Demand depends upon the choices individuals make, the margins by which they prefer some things to others as shown by the way they spend their money. Supply depends upon the cost of producing goods—how much it costs to employ the workers and to use the tools they work on. And something will be produced whenever the extra amount people are prepared to pay for it equals the extra cost of producing it.

Wonderful graphs can be constructed from these theories with supply moving in one direction and demand moving in the other, with what is finally produced depending on where the two graphs meet. The trouble is, these graphs in reality explain nothing since they do not explain where supply and demand come from in the first place. On the demand side they do not explain why the desires of some people (rich landowners, property millionaires or heads of privatised industries) translate themselves into 'effective demand', ie demand backed up by hard cash, while the desperate needs of other people (the unemployed, the low paid, the hungry peoples of Africa and Latin America) are ignored. On the supply side they do not explain why things which are desperately needed are not produced when the resources for them exist in abundance.

'Marginalist' economists say the extent of people's incomes, and therefore the extent of their demand, depends on how much they each contribute to the production of wealth. People get paid, it is claimed, according to the extra value their work creates. But this begs the question, why do some people get paid ten or 20 times as much as others for their labour, and why do some people get paid who don't work at all but simply own wealth? What work does the shareholder or the moneylender do?

There is an easy answer, to this, say the economists. Not only labour but also capital is involved in producing things. And just as labour gets paid according to what it contributed to wealth creation, so does capital. Each 'factor of production' gets a 'reward' equal to its 'marginal output'.

In fact, this argument solves nothing—apart from making it easier for the owners of capital to have an easy conscience. It really amounts to saying that those who are rich deserve to get richer. It relies on a tautology—like saying that '2 equals 2' or 'a cat is a cat'. For if the economists are asked how you measure the value of capital they refer to the 'marginal output' that capital produces. But if you ask them how you measure this 'marginal output' they refer to the value of the capital used up in producing it. They end up saying, in effect, 'The value of capital equals the value of capital', or, 'Profit equals profit'.

The only thing orthodox economics can say is that certain things are bought and certain things are sold at present, without saying why certain things are produced and not others, why some people are rich and some poor, and why some goods pile up unsold while people who desperately need them go without. Orthodox economists cannot tell us why sometimes there are booms and other times slumps.

These points were made against marginalist economics more than 80 years ago by the Austrian Marxist Rudolf Hilferding and the Russian revolutionary Nicolai Bukharin. They have been made again more recently in a rigorously logical form by dissident academic economists known as the 'Cambridge school'.

There are many other absurdities at the heart of orthodox economics. Its model of the market assumes perfect knowledge of all economic transactions, not only in the present but also in the future—a logical impossibility. It uses the 'theory of comparative advantage' borrowed from the early 19th century economist David Ricardo to preach unlimited free trade to the world's poorest countries—but the original theory was developed when capital did not have today's freedom to move from country to country. It insists that if the state does not interfere then supply and demand will automatically balance—but its own equations show that not to be the case. Finally, orthodox economics insists that if the multiple factors which obstruct free competition in the real world— whether the monopoly powers of giant companies or trade unionists defending jobs—are removed things must get better. But the mathematics of their model actually show that removing one restraint but not others can actually make things worse.

In fact the model offers no guidance to what is happening and what can happen in the real world. As one of the dissident economists, Paul Ormerod, pointed out in his *Death of Economics*, the orthodox wisdom is as much use in understanding the economy as medieval astrology was in predicting events. Economists who based themselves on the orthodoxy have completely failed to foresee the ups and downs of the world economy:

> Economic forecasts are the subject of open derision. Throughout the Western world their accuracy is appalling. Within the last 12 months alone, as this book is being written, they have failed to predict the Japanese recession, the strength of the American recovery, the depth of the collapse of the German economy, the turmoil in the European ERM.

Yet the orthodoxy continues to be taught in schools, to be studied in universities and to be thrown in the face of anyone who suggests there might be an alternative to the existing system of market capitalism. Its basic contention, that the market is the only rational way to organise production, has been accepted in recent

13

years not merely by the traditional right but by the leaders of the world's Labour, social democratic and former Communist parties.

Such an acceptance is only possible if you do not challenge the absurdities of the world. The orthodoxy rests on taking the world at face value, on saying that things are as they are because they are as they are. But it is of no use to those who find life in the existing world increasingly intolerable, who want an alternative to long slumps interspersed with short booms, to rising unemployment and deepening poverty, to goods that cannot be sold on the one hand and people who cannot afford to buy them on the other. To come to terms with these problems you need a different approach.

2 Explaining the topsy-turvy world

Karl Marx's approach to economics was very different to today's orthodoxy. He became interested in economics because he could see the inhuman absurdity of the new economic system—capitalism—then growing around him in Germany in the mid-1840s. He could already see it was a society in which people were continually being told to work harder in order to produce wealth, but reaping no benefit from their efforts. As he put it in 1844:

> The more the worker produces, the less he has to consume. The more value he creates, the more valueless, the more unworthy he becomes... [The system] replaces labour by machines, but it throws one section of workers back to a barbarous type of labour, and it turns the other section into a machine... It produces intelligence—but for the worker, stupidity... It produces palaces—but for the worker, hovels. It produces beauty—but for the worker, deformity... The worker only feels himself outside his work, and in his work feels outside himself. He feels at home when he is not working, when he is working he does not feel at home.

Four years later he wrote:

> The worker works in order to live. He does not even reckon labour as part of his life, but rather a sacrifice of his life... What he produces for himself is not the silk that he weaves, not the gold that he draws from the mine, not the palace that he builds. What he produces for himself are wages, and the silk, gold and palace resolve

themselves for him into a definite quantity of the means of sub-
sistence, perhaps into a cotton jacket, some copper coins and a
lodging in a cellar...

And the worker who for 12 hours weaves, spins, drills, turns,
builds, shovels, breaks stones, carries loads, etc—does he con-
sider this 12 hours weaving, spinning, drilling, turning, building,
shovelling, stone-breaking as a manifestation of his life, as life?
On the contrary, life begins for him when this activity ceases, at
the table, in the public house, in bed.

Marx's economic writings are about how this form of society
came into being and perpetuates itself. As such they are also writings about what established academic thinkers refer to as 'philosophy', 'sociology' and 'history'. They are not mainly about how
things have one price rather than another, nor even about why
and when economic crises take place. Rather, they are about the
whole world of 'alienated labour'—a world in which human
activity takes on a life of its own and dominates human beings
themselves, a world of endless work and unemployment, overproduction and starvation.

In his earliest writings Marx stressed the absurdity of this
upside down world. The word he used to describe this, 'alienation', came from the German philosopher Hegel, whose own
writings are often somewhat obscure. But Marx also based himself on various other sources. He used the accounts of the capitalist economic system to be found in the writings of founders of
orthodox capitalist economics like Adam Smith and David
Ricardo. And he drew on the experience of the first workers'
movements to fight back against this system, including the
Chartists in Britain.

In Marx's later economic writings, especially his three volume
work *Capital* he dropped much of the philosophical language.
This has led some people to claim that his whole approach to
economics had changed. In fact the aim of *Capital* is to explain
the way in which the whole world of 'alienated labour' develops,
as an inhuman force dominating living human beings. This is
clear from the notebooks Marx wrote immediately before com-
piling the final draft of *Capital*. Thus, he tells:

The rule of the capitalist over the worker is the rule of the object
over the human, of dead labour over living, of the product over the
producer, since in fact the commodities which become the means

of domination over the worker are...the products of the production process... It is the *alienation process* of his own social labour.

He makes the point that the capitalist system restricts both what the individual capitalist and the individual worker can do. But while 'the worker, as its victim, stands from the beginning in a relation of rebellion towards it and perceives the process as enslavement', the capitalist 'is rooted in the alienation process and finds in it his highest satisfaction...The self expansion of capital is the determining, dominating and overmastering purpose for the capitalist, the absolute driving force and component of his action...'

3 Production and commodities

You cannot understand any society, Marx pointed out, unless you look at how the people in that society get hold of the things they need to survive—their food, shelter and clothing. For, until they have a sure supply of them, they can do nothing else.

But getting these things has always depended on humans cooperating to change the natural world around them. Unlike other animal species, we are not equipped with special teeth or claws that enable us to kill wild animals or chew raw vegetation. We don't have fur to keep us warm. The only way humans can live and protect themselves from the vicissitudes of nature is by working to change it. As Engels put it, 'Labour is the source of all wealth, next to nature... But it is even infinitely more than this. It is the prime basic condition for all human existence.'

Historically, human labour has taken a variety of forms. For many tens of thousands of years it involved men and women working and living together in bands of about 40, collecting plant fruit and roots and killing wild animals. They were able to do this without rulers or male dominance over women. Then, about 10,000 years ago, it began, in different parts of the world, to involve the planting of crops and the domestication of animals. But the organisation of labour still did not involve one group in society lounging around in idleness while everyone else toiled. There was still a rough equality between all men and women, with a distribution of food, shelter and clothing according to people's needs—a state of affairs that persisted in many parts of the world right through to the colonial conquests of the last century.

In these societies there is no sign of the 'selfish', 'grasping', 'competitive' 'human nature' we take for granted under capitalism. Thus an early 18th century observer of the Iroquois cultivators noted:

> If a cabin of hungry Iroquois meets another whose provisions are not entirely exhausted, the latter share with the newcomers the little which remains to them without waiting to be asked, although they expose themselves thereby to the same dangers of perishing as those whom they help...

Of another group, the Montagnais, a Jesuit priest noted:

> Ambition and avarice do not exist in the great forests...as they are contented with a mere living, not one of them has given himself to the devil to acquire wealth.

And a classic study of the Nuer cattle keepers of East Africa reports that, 'In general it can be said that no-one in a Nuer village starves unless all are starving.'

It was only about 5,000 years ago that the class divide and the domination of women by men arose anywhere. This was a result of further change in the ways people produced their livelihoods, involving heavy agriculture, the smelting of metals and the building of the first towns. Exploiting classes emerged that lived off the labour of the rest of society and established states—permanent bodies of armed men organised as armies and police forces—to preserve and extend their rule.

Sometimes, as in early Ancient Egypt, in Ancient Mesopotamia and the Inca empire of South America, the ruling classes used the direct force of the state to seize the wealth created by those who worked in the form of taxes. Sometimes, as in Ancient Greece and Rome, they owned slaves who did all the work. Sometimes, as in Europe in the Middle Ages, they controlled the land and forced those who worked on it either to labour for them for nothing or to give them half or more of its output. But in each case a minority lived by forcing the majority of society to work for them.

In all of these societies, however, there was one thing in common with the egalitarian societies that had gone before. The goal of work was the immediate satisfaction of people's needs—although now the needs of a ruling minority took priority over those of the great majority of people. The slave, peasant or handicraft worker toiled to produce goods which would immediately be used either by themselves or by those who lived off their backs. So if the slave owner ate too much, or built himself too grandiose a palace or tomb, the slave would not have enough to live on and would go hungry. If the crop was not very good one year and the feudal lord insisted on living in luxury, the feudal peasant would starve. But what was impossible was a situation in which people would go hungry, as under the present system, because 'too much' was being produced. Production was *for use*—even if to a large extent for the use of one class which exploited everybody else. For this reason, Marx followed other economists in calling it the production of 'use values'.

However, in the society we live in today, capitalism, very little production is for immediate use. Car workers do not produce vehicles for their own immediate use, or even for the immediate use of their managing director. They produce cars so that their employer can sell them to someone else. The same is true for the steel worker, shoe operative, film technician, computer programmer, or, in fact, virtually anyone involved in paid work. You could, for example, spend all your life making screws, turning out tens of thousands a day by working on a machine. Yet you would probably never use more than a few hundred personally.

Goods are produced to be sold. They are 'commodities' that have to be exchanged for money before the producers get any benefit from their effort. Of course, eventually the goods have to be of use. But they have to be exchanged first.

So goods under capitalism have a strange peculiarity. Before they can be used, be 'use values', they have to be exchanged against money which in turn can then be exchanged for other goods. And you measure their value in terms of how much you get for them when you exchange them. What is key is 'exchange value'—how much money, and therefore how many other goods, you can get for your goods.

Through exchange, the effort put in by one individual is linked to that of millions of other individuals through the world system. This becomes obvious when you look at what you buy with the money you get for what you yourself produce. Say you buy a basket full of groceries from Tesco's—you have bread baked with wheat from Canada, apples and pears from South Africa or New Zealand, rabbit from China, tins of anchovies from Peru, flowers from Kenya, tin from Malaya or Bolivia, iron from the Great Lakes smelted in Germany, plastic wrapping made from oil from

Saudi Arabia or Kuwait. Any individual is thus linked to a system using the labour of people right across the world.

These worldwide linkages between the labour of many thousands of different people exist, despite the fact that there is no conscious coordination between them. They all work for different competing firms in different competing countries. Yet it is as if their labours were pooled together. There is a world system of production, but it is organised through the blind competition of individual firms, or, to use Marx's phrase, there is 'social production but individual appropriation'.

4 Labour and wealth

Economists before Marx had begun to provide an account of this system. They referred to the 'invisible hand' tying the activities of people together. They had also noted something else, that Marx accepted. All commodities have one thing in common. They are all the product of human labour.

Marx in *Capital* asks what it is that two very different objects that cost the same amount of money have in common—say a pair of socks and a loaf of bread. It is not their physical characteristics. They weigh different amounts, they are made up of different molecules, have different shapes and so on. Nor is it the use we finally make of them. You don't normally wear a loaf of bread or eat a pair of socks. Comparing the use to which we eventually put bread with the use to which we eventually put a sock is like comparing the weight of an elephant with the colour of the sky –they are completely different things. Instead, Marx argued, what the two have in common is the amount of labour that goes into making them. Further, it is this that actually determines their values.

This is easiest to understand when you have people making things to exchange among themselves. A carpenter might make a table and exchange it for a suit made by a tailor—but not if he could make a suit of the same quality in less time than it takes him to make the table. He reckons that the suit is worth at least the same number of hours of work as his table.

The same principle applies when people make things and sell them for money. The carpenter will sell a table which takes him say four hours to make for the sum of money that will enable him to buy something else which takes four hours to make. The

19

price of the table expresses the amount of labour that went into making it.

Of course, not all carpenters will be skilled enough to do the requisite job in four hours. Some will take twice as long (as I would if I was trying to make a table). But no one will be prepared to pay them the equivalent of eight hours work for the table, when someone else will supply it for the equivalent of four hours work. The price of the table expresses not the amount of work done by any particular individual, but the amount of labour required by an individual of average skill.

Through exchange, each individual's labour is continually compared with labour throughout the system as a whole. Or, as Karl Marx put it, the 'concrete labour' of each individual is measured as a portion of the 'social labour' of society as a whole.

Marx did not originate the view that labour was the ultimate source of value. This was accepted, at least in part, by many of the first economists to identify with the rising capitalist system, from John Locke at the close of the 17th century, through Adam Smith in the 18th century to David Ricardo in the early 19th century. Thus Adam Smith argued:

> The real price of everything, what it really costs the men who want to acquire it, is the toil and trouble of acquiring it... It is not by gold or silver, but by labour, that all the wealth of the world was originally purchased, and its value to those who possess it and who want to exchange it for some other object, is precisely equal to the quantity of labour which it enables them to purchase or command.

But pro-capitalist proponents of any such 'labour theory of value' have always run into an almost insuperable problem. If labour is the source of value, how does profit arise?

If all goods are exchanged according to the amount of labour contained in them, then everyone in society should be on a more or less equal footing. Some might choose to work longer, and so get a little more wealth and a little less leisure. But people should lead equally satisfactory lives. Again some people might be less skilled and lose out at first, but over time they should catch up. So where could systematic profit making come from? Individuals might make a profit by fiddling other individuals. But this could not explain how there was a whole class of rich people—and, indeed, under modern capitalism nearly all those who actually sell goods are rich.

As Marx pointed out:

> The class of capitalists taken as a whole cannot enrich itself as a class, it cannot increase its total capital…by one capitalist gaining what another loses. The class as a whole cannot defraud itself.

But if capitalists do not get their profits from each other, then they must get them from elsewhere. But where?

Already, nearly 100 years before Marx, Adam Smith had tried to explain profit by mixing his view of labour as the source of value with another view, which saw capital as adding to value by producing a 'revenue'.

Now some forms of capital—machines, factory buildings and so on—do make labour much more productive than it would be otherwise. Even the most elementary tool adds enormously to human productivity: a labourer with a wheelbarrow can move a much bigger weight with less effort than someone carrying things on their back. But machines and factory buildings are not things that exist in their own right. They are the product of previous human labour. The wheel barrow which aids the toil of the labourer is itself the product of the toil of the metal worker. That was why Marx called the means of production 'dead labour' (as opposed to present work, which is 'living labour').

The value of goods on sale still depends on the labour that goes into them, although some of that is past rather than present labour. If a capitalist says he should be rewarded for making an investment in plant or machinery, he has to be asked how the plant or machinery got into his hands, rather than into the hands of those whose labour first made it. What is more, there is no way that a machine can add to the value of something without being worked on by living labour. A machine by itself does nothing. It is the human being operating the machine that causes it to turn out new goods, with an increased value.

The human being can make things without the machine. The machine cannot make anything without the human being setting it to work.

The fact that it is human labour that ultimately determines the exchange value of things is shown by what happens with modern technological advance. Items that used to be very expensive 20 or 30 years ago have fallen in price as technological advance has reduced the amount of labour needed to produce them, even

21

though the machines involved in their production have often got more complex and expensive. So an electro-mechanical adding machine used to cost £40 or £50 in the 1960s (equivalent to £400 or £500 in terms of today's money), but you can buy an electronic calculator with greater power today for £1 or £2. Similarly, a medium powered computer would have cost you half a million pounds then. Now you can get one of similar power for £600 or £700.

The goods which have not fallen in price in this way are the goods that still require nearly as much labour to produce as in the past—cars, food and drink, bricks and mortar, and much clothing.

5 Profit and exploitation

The idea that labour is the source of all value, including that which goes to the capitalist as profit, interest and rent became increasingly embarrassing to apologists for capitalism after the time of Adam Smith. It implied that the capitalists were just as big parasites as the feudalists they replaced. This led pro-capitalist economists to develop different theories based on 'abstinence' to explain profit. Profits, they now claimed, were a reward to the capitalist for using his wealth to employ people rather than for his own immediate consumption.

But as Marx pointed out, this is absurd. Employing people involves buying their labour. If a capitalist gets a profit for doing this, then everyone else who buys something should get a profit. So why don't workers get a profit when they buy the things they need to live on?

The abstinence theory is pure mythology. The capitalist does not sacrifice his existing wealth when he invests. In fact, his investment preserves its worth, while profit is something he gets on top for doing nothing.

So if real profit rates are 10 percent (quite a low figure by capitalist standards) someone with a million pounds to invest can spend £100,000 a year (£2,000 a week) on indulging themselves in the most unabstemious way and still be worth as much at the end of the year as at the beginning—and get another £100,000 the next year for doing nothing. By contrast, even if a worker earning today's average 1995 wage was able, miraculously, to 'abstain' from food, shelter and clothing completely, it would take him or her 80 years to earn enough to make such an investment.

What is really happening, Marx insisted, is that the capitalist is able to make a profit by seizing some of the labour of his workers, just as the slave owner could enjoy a life of luxury by forcing slaves to toil for him and the feudal lord could fill his belly by making the peasant work on his estate for nothing. The only difference is that there was nothing to conceal from slaves or the medieval peasants the all too harsh reality that the fruits of their labour were being taken by someone else. They knew it because someone stood over them with a whip or cudgel.

By contrast, there seems to be a fair and equal exchange between the worker and the capitalist under the present system. Workers sell their labour for a sum of money—their wages. And what they get depends on the going rate for the job much as what the greengrocer gets for eggs depends on the current price. There is, it seems, 'a fair day's work for a fair day's pay'.

But this apparently 'fair' exchange between the worker and the capitalist disguises a fundamental inequality between them. Both have the ability to work (although the capitalist hardly ever has to use this ability). But only one of them, the capitalist, has control of the tools and the materials which are required for work to go ahead. But if people do not have access to tools or land then they are faced with the grim choice of going hungry or of working for those individuals who do own tools or land.

As Adam Smith pointed out:

> In the original state of things, which precedes both the appropriation of land and the accumulation of stock, the whole product of labour belonged to the labourer... But as soon as the land becomes private property, the landowner demands a share of the produce...
>
> The produce of all labour is liable to a like deduction of profit... In all...manufactures the greater part of the workmen stand in need of a master to advance them the materials of their work... He shares in the product of their labour.

What was true in Adam Smith's day, when many small farmers and self employed artisans still owned the means for making a living on their own behalf, is a hundred times truer today. All the means for making wealth—the factories, the machines, the agricultural land—are in the hands of a very small number of people. In Britain 200 top companies, run by an interlocking group of some 800 directors, control the means of production responsible for turning out over half the national product. The great bulk of the 24 million strong workforce in Britain have no choice but to seek to work for such people. This applies not merely to the manual workers who are usually identified as the 'working class'. It also applies to very many white collar employees who think of themselves as 'middle class'. Filing clerks, computer operators, subeditors on magazines and newspapers or shop assistants are all forced to sell their labour just as much as car workers or dockers.

Very few people who leave school or who are made redundant have the means to set themselves up in business on their own. The only alternative to trying to sell their labour to the firms owning factories and offices is to try to live on the pittance provided by the welfare system. Even this amount is increasingly restricted by governments which speak of the need to give people an 'incentive' to work.

The harsh reality is that the great mass of the population cannot dream of leading even a half decent life unless they are prepared to sell their labour to those who control the means of production. They may be 'free' in the sense that they do not have to work for any one individual firm or capitalist. But they cannot escape having to try to work for someone.

As Marx put it, 'the worker can leave the individual capitalist to whom he hires himself whenever he likes... But the worker, whose sole source of livelihood is the sale of his labour, cannot leave the whole class of purchasers, that is the capitalist class, without renouncing his existence. He belongs not to this or that bourgeois, but to the bourgeois class.'

The worker may not be a slave, the personal property of one capitalist. But he or she is a 'wage slave', compelled to toil for some member of the class of capitalists. This puts the worker in a position where he or she has to accept a wage less than the total product of their labour. The value of their wage under capitalism is never nearly as big as the value of the labour they actually do.

6 Where profit comes from

In everyday language we often say that workers are paid 'for their labour'. But Marx pointed out that the phrase 'their labour' means two different things.

It means *the labour they do*, but it also means *their capacity to work*—which he baptised 'labour power'.

The two things are very different. People's capacity to work depends on them getting enough food, shelter, clothing and rest time to enable them to arrive at work each day fresh enough to put in the required effort and pay sufficient attention to the tasks facing them. They will be physically incapable of work unless they get paid enough to buy these things. As Adam Smith noted:

> There is a certain minimum below which it is impossible to reduce for any considerable time the ordinary wages of even the lowest species of labour. A man must always live by his work, and his wages must be enough to maintain him. They must even on most occasions be somewhat more; otherwise it would be impossible for him to bring up his family and the race of such workmen could not last beyond the first generation.

Exactly what counts as 'enough' for workers depends on the job they do and the general conditions in the society in which they live. So workers in Western Europe, the US, Japan or even South Korea today normally expect to get better food, shelter and clothing and more rest time than did the Manchester workers Engels met in the mid-1840s—or, for that matter, many workers in India or Africa today. And the more farsighted employer sometimes recognises that he must provide his workers with certain minimum conditions if they are to toil productively, just as the clever farmer knows he has to give his cows an adequate amount of hay if he is to get a high milk yield. An article in the *Financial Times* in January 1995 reported, 'Many managers realise…that unless their staff take their holidays and maintain a life outside work they will fail to perform effectively. "I insist on my staff taking their holidays," explained a partner at one leading British accountancy firm. "Otherwise they become less productive".'

Of course, many employers do not see it like this. They resent every penny they spend on wages and every minute workers are not toiling for them. And the workers certainly do not see their wage as being just a means to enable them to work for the employer. They see it as something which gives them the chance to buy what they want—whether it is a few pints of beer, a secondhand car, toys for the kids, or a couple of weeks holiday. That is why there is always a continual struggle between employers and workers, with employers trying to force wages down below the minimum needed to sustain the lives of the workers' families, and the workers trying to force wages above this minimum, to give themselves a little more 'free time' and a few 'little luxuries'.

But the reality under capitalism today, just as much as in Marx's time, is that the mass of manual and white collar workers are physically or mentally exhausted when they finish work, spending their money on things that do little more than restore them to a condition to resume work the next day or the next week. You don't see many manual or white collar workers who are not tired when they crowd into the buses or trains to work in the morning, or when they crowd into them again to return home in the evening.

The wage or salary the worker gets depends on the cost of restoring this capacity to work—the cost of replenishing 'labour power'. If wages are too low, workers will be ill nourished and too tired to work adequately. They won't want to work and the capitalist won't be able to get as much production out of them as he wants. If, on the other hand, the wage is greater than the cost of restoring the workers' capacity to toil, the employer will do his utmost to replace them with other workers he can get more cheaply.

Just as with any other good that is bought and sold, the value of the worker's labour power depends on how much labour is needed to produce it. That is, it depends on how much labour goes into producing the sustenance needed to keep the worker fit, healthy and ready to work—how much is needed to provide three meals a day, transport to work, a little relaxation in the evenings and at weekends, the upbringing of children who become the next generation of workers. But the amount of labour required to produce the goods that make you fit and able for work is not the same as the amount you can actually do once you start working. It may only take four person hours of society's total labour to produce your family's food, shelter and clothing. But you are capable, under pressure, of putting in eight, ten or even 12 hours a day. And the capitalist will refuse to pay you your wage unless you do so.

He pays you the going rate for your labour power. But he gets from you *a day's labour*—and that is worth much more than the going rate for *a day's labour power*.

So if it takes four hours work to produce the goods you live on but you work an eight hour day, then the capitalist is taking four hours work a day off you for nothing.

Because he controls the means of production he is able to

pocket a surplus of four labour hours a day. This surplus Marx called 'surplus value'—the source of profit, interest and rent.

The capitalist grabs this value off the worker every day. And by doing so, he continually puts himself in a position to grab still more surplus value. For the surplus value provides him with the wherewithal to get further means of production and to force workers to slave for him in future.

Yet, after all this has happened, the capitalists claim they are doing the workers a favour by allowing them to work. They claim they are the 'work providers', as if no social labour could take place without their prior robbery. And some people within the working class movement are stupid enough to refer to them as 'partners in production', as if the slave owner is the 'partner' of the slave or the feudal lord the 'partner' of the feudal serf.

The reality is that, each time the worker works, he adds to the control which the capitalist exercises. This is true even if conditions are such as to allow an improvement in the workers' living standards. As Marx puts it in *Capital*:

> Just as little as better clothing, food and treatment do away with
> the exploitation of the slave, so little do they set aside that of the
> wage worker. A rise in the price of labour only means that the
> length and weight of the golden chain the wage worker has already
> forged for himself allow of a relaxation of the tension of it.

This enables the capitalists to get into their hands all the plant machinery and raw materials needed for further production. They can then pretend to be the 'wealth creators', the people who 'provide work' for others. In fact, what they have done is steal the product of the labour of others—and then forbid it to be used for further production unless they are allowed to steal again.

7 Robbery and the rise of capitalism

Today we take the buying and selling of labour power for granted. It seems as 'natural' as the rising and setting of the sun. Yet it was nowhere more than a minor feature of any society until a few hundred years ago. In Europe in the late Middle Ages or in Africa and Asia at the time of European colonisation in the 18th and 19th centuries most people had some direct access to the means of getting a livelihood—even if they had to hand over a slice of what they produced to a parasitic landlord. Peasants could grow food on their own land. Craftsmen could make goods in their own little workshops.

What changed this was a primeval act of robbery—the use of force to remove masses of people from any control over the means of production. This was carried through by the forces of the state at the behest of some of the most privileged groups in society.

So in England and Wales, for example, the rise of capitalism was accompanied by 'enclosures'—a series of acts of parliament which forcibly drove peasants from common land they had cultivated for centuries. Further laws were then passed against 'vagrancy', which compelled the dispossessed peasants to seek work at whatever wage they could get. In Scotland the 'clearances' had the same effect, as the lairds drove the crofters (small farmers) from the land so as to replace them first by sheep and then by deer.

As Britain's rulers carved out an empire for themselves throughout the rest of the world, they took measures to bring about the same separation of the mass of people from control over the means of gaining a livelihood. In India they granted complete ownership of the land to the already highly privileged zamindar class. In East and South Africa they usually forced each household to pay a fixed sum of money, the poll tax, which it could only raise by sending some of its members to seek employment with European ranchers or businessmen. And in North America and the Caribbean when they found they could not force the indigenous population to become 'free' wage labour they imported millions of slaves kidnapped from West Africa to provide the profits they wanted.

Marx called this process of creating the conditions for the growth of capitalist production 'the primitive accumulation of capital'. It involved two things—on the one hand, the concentration of massive wealth in the hands of the capitalist class, on the other the 'freeing' of the mass of population from any direct access to the means of making a livelihood.

Once capitalism had established itself, its own economic mechanisms pushed these processes further forward. Thus in Britain in the late 18th century there were still hundreds of thousands of handloom weavers, who worked for themselves weaving cloth to sell. Within 50 years they had all been driven out of business by capitalist firms using powerlooms. In Ireland in the 1840s a terrible famine caused by the requirement that hungry peasants pay rent to (mainly British) landlords—even after the potato harvest had failed—led a million to die of hunger and another million to abandon their holdings and seek work in Britain and the US.

The story has been repeated many times since. In Africa, Asia and Latin America routine 'economic' pressures—backed up by police action against those who cannot afford rents—have forced hundreds of millions of people to desert peasant holdings to seek work, often with little success, in the slums of great cities. There they have no choice but to toil for whatever wage they can get. Once capitalism is fully established in any part of the world, its need for direct force to make people work diminishes. Over time people forget that they were once able to make a livelihood without working for someone else. They begin to take for granted the relationship between the boss and the worker. And all too often they accept the capitalist message which disguises the reality of wage slavery behind talk of capitalists 'providing work'.

The fact of exploitation—of a few people getting hold of value created by many—is hidden from view.

Marx used the term 'fetishism of commodities' to refer to such a situation. He pointed out that people make the mistake of only looking at what happens on the capitalist market, without seeing the real human relationships which underlie it. The conclusion is that there is no other way of organising things.

8 The dynamic of capitalism

Marxism is outdated, says Tony Blair, leader of the Labour Party, because, he claims, it does not understand the 'dynamism' of the 'market economy'.

Such a claim shows Tony Blair's ignorance about Marx's ideas. For Marx's whole analysis of capitalism was based on an understanding of the dynamism of the system—of its inability to stand still, of its relentless transformation of production and of the lives of those who worked within its system.

The *Communist Manifesto*, which Marx wrote with Frederick Engels early in 1848, insisted:

> The bourgeoisie, during its rule of scarce one hundred years, has created more massive and more colossal productive forces than all the preceding generations put together.

It emphasised the continual transformation of industry under   29 capitalism:

> The bourgeoisie cannot exist without constantly revolutionising the means of production... Constant revolutionising of production...distinguish the bourgeois epoch from all earlier ones.

In *Capital* Marx sees the continual drive to build up ever bigger industry as the characteristic feature of capitalism:

> Fanatically bent on making value expand itself, he [the capitalist] ruthlessly forces the human race to produce for production's sake... Accumulation for the sake of accumulation, production for production's sake!

Capital shows how this inbuilt obsession with accumulation arises from the very nature of the capitalist market. The work's first volume begins with analysing production for the market ('commodity production'), then looks what happens when wage labour arises and labour power becomes a commodity, and culminates in showing how production using wage labour brings about a process of compulsive accumulation that ignores human need and individual desires.

Marx's disagreement with Tony Blair and other allegedly 'modern', but in reality very old fashioned, pro-capitalist thinkers, is not because he fails to see capitalism as dynamic. It is because he sees, as they do not, that its dynamism is inseparable from its inhumanity and irrationality.

Capitalism is based on a system of social production, involving today a worldwide workforce of about three billion people. Yet the organisation of production is by separate, rival firms (most privately owned, some owned by rival national states), motivated only by the need to keep ahead of each other in competition. The fact that each firm is involved in exploiting wage labour means that none of them dare rest on its laurels. However successful a firm may have been in the past, it lives in fear of a rival firm investing profits in new and more modern plant and machinery. So every firm has to worry continually about keeping its profits ahead of its rivals. And that means every firm trying to get its workers to do as much as possible for as low wages as possible. No capitalist dare stand still for any length of time. That would mean falling behind the competitors and eventually going bust.

It is this which explains the dynamism of capitalism. The pressure on each capitalist to keep ahead of every other leads to continual upgrading of plant and machinery, and continual pressure on workers to provide the profits which make the upgrading possible. But it is this too which makes the system inhuman.

In a sane world the introduction of new labour saving equipment would lead automatically to higher living standards and a shorter working week. But not under capitalism, where each firm is intent on cutting its costs to stay in business—and that means trying to hold down workers' living standards.

The inhumanity and irrationality of decision making under capitalism are such that even the bosses are not free to do what they want. They can choose to exploit their workers in one way rather than another. But they cannot choose not to exploit their workers at all, or even to exploit them less than other capitalists do—unless they want to go bust. They themselves are subject to a system which pursues its relentless course whatever the feelings of individuals. Capitalism is indeed a rat race. Any capitalist who is not a rat, who tries to treat workers well, putting their needs above the drive to compete, does not last for long.

Furthermore, the blind competition between capitalists inevitably creates conditions which threaten to throw the whole system into chaos. The production of rival firms is linked by the market. No one capitalist can keep production up unless he sells his goods. But the ability to sell depends on the spending of other capitalists—on their direct spending on goods (as luxuries and as plant and machinery for their firms) and on the wages which they pay to the workers (who, in turn, spend them on their upkeep). But these capitalists cannot spend unless they have sold their own goods.

The market makes production anywhere in the system depend on what is happening everywhere else. If the chain of buying and selling breaks down at any point, the whole system can begin to grind to a halt. Then an economic crisis results.

CHAPTER 2

Explaining the crisis

9 Boom and slump

The history of industrial capitalism has been a history of booms and slumps—of what establishment economists call 'the business cycle'. For nearly 200 years there have been spells of frenetic expansion of production interspersed with sudden collapses, in which whole sections of industry grind to a halt.

We have been through three such recessions in the last 20 years, and each has imposed a heavier burden on those who work than the one before, with people's lives devastated as they have lost their livelihoods—and sometimes their homes as well. Such periodic crises are built into the way the system runs.

Each firm is out to maximise profits. If profits seem easy to make, then firms right through the system expand their output as rapidly as possible. They open up new factories and offices, buy new machinery and take on employees, believing they will find it easy to sell the goods that are turned out. As they do so, they provide a ready market for other firms, who can easily sell plant and machinery to them, or consumer goods to the workers they've employed. The whole economy booms, more goods are produced, unemployment falls.

But this can never last. A 'free' market means there is no coordination between the different competing firms. So, for example, the car manufacturers can decide to expand their output, without there being at the same time any necessary expansion by the firms that make steel for car bodies or the plantations in Malaysia that produce rubber for tyres. In the same way, firms can start taking on skilled workers, without any of them agreeing to undertake the necessary training to increase the total number of such workers.

All that matters to any of the firms is to make as much profit as possible as quickly as possible. But the blind rush to do so can easily lead to the using up of existing supplies of raw materials and components, skilled labour, and finance for industry.

In every boom that capitalism has ever experienced, a point has been reached at which shortages of raw materials, components, skilled labour and finance suddenly arise. Prices and interest rates begin to climb—and this in turn encourages workers to take action to protect their living standards.

The boom inevitably results in rising inflation. And, more seriously for the individual capitalists, rising costs quickly destroy the profits of some firms and force them to the edge of bankruptcy. The only way for them to protect themselves is to cut back production, sack workers and shut down plants. But in doing so they destroy the market for the goods of other firms. The boom gives way to a slump.

Suddenly there is 'overproduction'. Goods pile up in warehouses because people cannot afford to buy them. The workers who have produced them are sacked, since they cannot be sold. This means workers can buy fewer goods and the amount of 'overproduction' in the system as a whole actually gets greater.

The car industry cannot sell as many cars as in the past, so it buys less steel. As a result, steel plants are shut down and steel workers sacked. But the sacked steel workers cannot buy cars, and so fewer cars are produced. It is the turn of car workers to be sacked, but then they cannot buy things like washing machines or fridges made of steel, so less steel is required, more steel plants are shut, more steel workers are sacked and fewer cars can be bought. There is a vicious circle in which each firm claims it can only survive by holding down wages, pushing up productivity and sacking workers. But every time it does so, it means fewer

33

markets for other firms, more sackings and wage cuts there and eventually, a smaller market for its own goods.

The turn from boom to slump always takes big business by surprise. All through the late 1980s establishment figures on both sides of the Atlantic proclaimed that their economies were doing miraculously. In 1990 the British Tory prime minister, John Major, and his chancellor of the exchequer, Norman Lamont, proclaimed repeatedly that there would be no recession. Almost all the professional economic forecasters backed them up. 'The good news in the latest *Economic Outlook* from the Organisation for Economic Cooperation and Development is that economic activity in the industrialised world has settled to a sustainable 3 percent economic growth rate', reported Peter Norman in the *Financial Times*.

Then, as if from nowhere, the slump broke. The same Peter Norman now reported 'a litany of grim economic news. Practically all the indicators about declining output, falling retail sales and rising unemployment have been worse than expected'. The *Financial Times* itself was absolutely baffled as to what had happened. 'We are in the dark,' admitted one of its regular columnists. Lamont now spoke of recessions as if they were a natural phenomenon like the ebbing and flowing of the tide. His predecessor, Nigel Lawson, who had boasted most about the alleged 'economic miracle' of the 1980s now insisted, 'The economic cycle is a fact of life. There always have been and there always will be these ups and downs.'

As Marx noted, businessmen always think things are going wonderfully until the slump suddenly breaks: 'Business always appears thoroughly sound until suddenly the debacle takes place.' But break the slump always does. And it always leads to a massive devastation of people's lives and a massive waste of resources. Yet the response of employers and governments to the slump is always to tell people that there is 'not enough to go round', and that 'everyone has to make sacrifices' and 'tighten their belts'.

In the recession of the early 1990s the British economy produced in each year at least 6 percent less than it could have done—leading to a total loss of up to £36 billion of output each year for nearly three years. To put it another way, the loss each year was nearly as much as the cost of the National Health Service. The recession was less serious in the US than in Britain. Nevertheless, its output loss was more than 50 billion dollars per year. If it had grown modestly, there would have been an extra 150 billion dollars of output a year—a figure equal to that which the whole black population of sub-Saharan Africa have to live on.

And that is by no means an exhaustive account of the total waste involved. For this was not the first, but the third crisis the Western world had gone through in the previous 16 years. If the Western economies had been able to grow through these years at the same average speed as in the 20 years before, then total output would have been more than 40 percent higher than it was.

The waste resulting, worldwide, from economic crises is much greater than that caused by all the natural catastrophes— all the earthquakes, volcanic eruptions, floods and epidemics— combined. But economic crises are not natural disasters.

The means of producing the things people desperately need continue to exist just as much in the midst of an economic crisis as before—on the one side, the factories, mines, dockyards, fields, etc, capable of turning out goods, on the other the workers capable of labouring in them.

It is not some natural catastrophe which stops unemployed men and women working in the closed down industries, but the organisation of capitalism.

10 Capitalist economics and the economic crisis

Despite the waste and devastation of people's lives caused by capitalist crisis, most mainstream economists have tried to pretend that they do not really happen. They have followed a 'law' developed by a French economist who lived two centuries ago, Jean Baptiste Say. He said that crisis is impossible, since every time a good is sold by someone it is bought by someone else. This law is built into the 'marginalist' or 'neo-classical' school of economics today.

It claims 'the invisible hand' of the market automatically ensures that any goods produced can be bought, that 'supply' equals 'demand'. The prices of goods, it says, act as signals telling capitalists what to produce. This 'theory' underlies all the fashionable praise for markets by politicians throughout the world today. It is their justification for dismantling controls, privatising industries and declaring that socialism is 'out of date'.

The 'theory' is full of holes.

Price 'signals' can never relate output and demand, selling and buying, production and consumption, smoothly. Production is always a process taking place *in time*. 'Price signals' do not tell you what *will be* wanted when production is finished, but what *was* wanted before it began.

This time factor creates immense problems, even with the simplest forms of commodity production like the growing of grain by a mass of small farmers. If there is bad weather one year and the crop suffers, then prices do indeed rise. This cannot, however, cause more production of grain that year. In the real world (as opposed to the world of the market theorists) the farmers have to wait until the following spring to sow their next crop. They may respond to 'price signals' by sowing a bigger area than previously. But unless, by coincidence, one year of bad weather is followed by a second such year, the only result will be to produce more grain than consumers demand.

The best known such problem is called the 'pig cycle', because pig farmers repeatedly find that either the demand for pork exceeds the number of pigs they have ready to sell, or the number of pigs on their hands is much greater than the willingness of people to buy pork. But similar ups and downs have always beset every sort of agricultural production.

The cycles do not go away when you move from a world of small farmers to one of giant capitalist firms. In fact they get worse.

Industrial production does not begin just a few months ahead of final consumption. It depends upon making a huge investment in fixed capital, on building factories and installing machinery, over several years. Since there is a 'free market' there can be no coordination between rival firms. And so alternations of 'over-production' and 'excess demand', of slump and boom, are even more pronounced than in a purely agricultural system.

The only way for the orthodoxy to get round the problem is to ignore it. This was openly recognised by one of the founders of 'marginalism', Leon Walras. 'We shall resolve this difficulty', he wrote, 'purely and simply by ignoring the time element at this point'. Roy Radner, an economist who set out in the late 1960s to prove mathematically that the competitive market economy would produce an equilibrium—a stable balance between what was produced and what was required—was forced to conclude that this was impossible. For it assumed that those involved in the system would have to work out, in advance, how they would respond to all the possibilities facing them at any point in the future. The model of a perfect balance, he concluded, 'breaks down completely' faced with the impossibility of people doing so.

In fact, in the real world, if an equilibrium is eventually reached between production and consumption, it is not by a smooth, efficient, painless fitting together of supply and demand, but by violent convulsion—the slump.

Two schools of pro-capitalist economists have recognised this.

The great crisis of the 1930s led some economists, most notably John Maynard Keynes, to reject the crude version of Say's law. Keynes was a supporter of capitalism—he himself made a fortune speculating on the stock exchange—but he wanted to save it from itself. He accepted much of the theoretical framework of the dominant 'marginalist' economics. But if the system were left to itself, he argued, slumps would occur in which both the market for goods and the output of them fell, so that 'supply' and 'demand' were only equal to each other because both were at a very low level. This led him to reject the conventional wisdom of his day— and of our day more than 60 years later—that the economy would automatically blossom if only governments stopped 'poking their noses' into the economy. Keynes held, to the contrary, that only government intervention could stop slumps.

In the 1940s, 1950s and 1960s such views were incorporated into an amended version of 'marginalism' to become the orthodoxy accepted by governments of all complexions and taught to economics students. John Samuelson, the Nobel prize winner who wrote the best selling economics textbook of the time, boasted in it that slumps would never happen again: 'The National Bureau of Economic Research has worked itself out of one of its first jobs, namely business cycles.'

Such faith in government intervention in the system did not survive the big recession of 1974-76. Virtually overnight economists and politicians who had preached the Keynesian doctrine for 30 years suddenly changed their minds. As the American economists Mankiw and Romer have pointed out, the 'Keynesian consensus' was replaced by a return to the old idea 'that markets always clear' and that 'the invisible hand always guides the economy to the efficient allocation of resources'.

Economists and politicians now embraced, to varying degrees, a doctrine called 'monetarism'. This held that, far from government

37

intervention being necessary, governments should not intervene, except to keep in check the total amount of money in the economy and to stop 'unnatural monopolies', like that which trade unions were said to exert when they defended living standards.

The triumphal return of the old orthodoxy in the late 1970s and 1980s was marked by a return of the assumption that the market always brought supply and demand together perfectly. This confidence was most fully articulated by the Thatcher wing of the Tory Party in Britain and by those who embraced similar ideas in the former Eastern bloc and the Third World. But it was also echoed by many who used to be on the left.

But there was a barely noticed contradiction within the ideas of the Thatcherites themselves. For they were very much under the influence of a second dissident school, the so called 'Austrian school' whose best known figure was Friedrich Hayek. He had always opposed Keynesianism and state intervention, on the grounds that this produced 'tyranny' and undermined the 'dynamism' of the market. But he had never accepted the neo-classical, marginalist scheme, with its denial of crisis. He recognised that the system was inevitably prone to destructive ups and downs, referring to 'equilibrium' as 'a somewhat unfortunate term'.

Hayek also accepted that the market often produces the opposite of what people want. 'Competition is only valid in so far as its results are unpredictable, and on the whole differ from those which anyone has, or could have, deliberately aimed at.' 'Spontaneous order produced by the market does not ensure that what general opinion regards as the most important needs are always met before the less important ones.'

Hayek at his most frank insisted that the market did not lead to a smooth balance between supply and demand, but proceeded through what his fellow 'Austrian' Joseph Schumpeter called 'creative destruction', resulting not in an economic equilibrium but an economic 'order'.

This is not, however, a very palatable economic doctrine for politicians seeking votes or ideologists seeking converts. After all, the 'creative destruction' is of the livelihoods—and sometimes the lives—of millions of people. So the version of Hayek's ideas that is usually preached today is a hybrid version, in which the 'neo-classical' notion of a smooth equilibrium replaces the idea of 'creative destruction'.

The image we are presented with is that instant prosperity will follow if only people embrace the market without reservations.

This is what people in the former Eastern bloc were promised after the old Stalinist economies entered into deep crisis in the late 1980s. The market, they were told, would bring about 'economic miracles' such as West Germany had allegedly experienced in the 1950s and 1960s—and would do so in '400 or 500' days.

The same message has been handed out by the International Monetary Fund to some 60 or 70 'third world' countries with its 'structural adjustment programmes'. And the British Tory party's main message in the 1992 general election was no different. The economic recovery would start, it promised, the moment it was returned to power with its programme of spreading the market still wider.

In each case the reality that followed was not equilibrium, but destruction. In the case of the East European countries it meant destruction of between 20 and 40 percent of industry through the worst slumps history has known. In the countries of Africa there were massive cutbacks in people's living standards as a continent that had been able to feed all its people 20 years before became home to millions of starving. In the case of Britain, it meant the worst slump since the 1930s.

11 How the crisis breaks

Enthusiasm for the allegedly miraculous powers of the market is usually greatest during booms. As profits grow, capitalists stampede past each other in the rush to produce more and more goods. Some of the wealth the very rich control spills over into the hands of those just below them. Contractors make profits erecting new warehouses, factories and offices. Advertising agencies find an apparently unlimited demand for their services. Estate agents prosper as properties change hands at growing speed. Whole sections of the middle class feel that they only have to set up in business on their own and money will drop into their laps.

All of these groups buy growing numbers of goods themselves, creating a rising demand for luxuries from champagne and caviar to porsches and penthouse suites. They also add to the demand for the labour of the mass of workers, as there are more jobs in building sites and car showrooms, estate agents and travel agents, banks and finance houses, in taking down tele-ads and in printing advertising supplements. These new workers find they can buy things they were not able to afford—and this, in turn, leads to more demand for the things produced by a whole range of other workers, from those in car and textile factories to those in fast food outlets and DIY shops.

Eventually unemployment falls—even if, as today, it is still not as low as it once was. Employers, desperate to employ particular grades of skilled workers, bid against each other for them and push wages up a little. Other workers, less frightened by the threat of redundancy, begin to demand their share of the 'prosperity' they hear about from the media and put in wage claims which employers sometimes feel they have to concede.

At the bottom of society very wide numbers of people still do not notice any real improvement in their position. Even workers who get wage increases find these do not compensate for rising prices. But for a brief moment the claim that the market equals prosperity seems, to anyone who does not look beneath the surface of events, to correspond to reality.

All the factors that turn the boom into a slump are already developing when the boom is at its height—rising prices, a growing shortage of finance for new investment, an upward movement of some skilled workers' wages. But they are concealed by the frenetic character of the boom. Indeed, even as they begin to cut into some profits, they can lead to a rise in speculation, and a feverish race to grab still more profit. Capitalists who believe that there are never ending opportunities for profit switch their money from one sector to another at great speed—buying raw materials on the assumption that they will be able to sell them at a higher price, financing office building in the expectation of ever rising rents, swinging behind the latest advertising venture, pouring huge sums into the stock exchange on the assumption that share prices can never fall. Even workers can get pulled into the speculative orgy, borrowing to the eyeballs to buy houses in the belief that their price will rise.

Crooks and conmen of all sorts prosper in this get rich quick atmosphere. Any small scale crook who hawks an enterprise that promises rapid profit, however disreputable the project, is bound to find some buyers. And the giant capitalist who wants to become even bigger by fiddling the books to finance a takeover bid finds it easy to do so.

In this glistening atmosphere, as money seems to rain down on the champagne drinking classes, any connection between the glorious business of raking in profit and the murky business of exploitation in the workplace seems to be lost. So it was, for instance, in Britain in the late 1980s, as the Murdochs and the Maxwells, the Hansons and the Reichman Brothers reigned supreme. Those who had dedicated their lives to the profit system believed their time had come.

Such was the power of the most recent capitalist boom that even some of those who in the past had opposed the system were won over to it. Marxism was condemned on all sides as irrelevant and even a magazine that called itself *Marxism Today* revelled in the upper middle class fashion for expensive clothes and the delights of mixing with Tory cabinet ministers. We were, it was said, in a post-Marxist world—post-industrial, post-mass production, post-crisis and postmodern.

Then, quite predictably for those who were not 'post-Marxists', the crisis struck. One after another the great names of the 1980s went bust—B and C, Coloroll, Canary Wharf, Habitat, Maxwell, eventually the post-Marxist *Marxism Today*.

The tone of the media suddenly changed. Those who had used the business pages of the posh papers to toast the boom now suddenly announced that the system was on 'the edge of a precipice', that it was going down and no-one could see the bottom.

This has always happened when boom has turned to bust. So, for instance, the American steel magnate Andrew Carnegie could write in the 1880s:

> Manufacturers...see the savings of many years...becoming less and less, with no hope of change in the situation. It is in a soil thus prepared that anything promising relief is gladly welcomed. The manufacturer is in the position of patients who have tried in vain every doctor for years...

This was once more the tone in the early 1930s, where despair was nearly universal in Germany and the US.

At such times economists and journalists who previously accepted the wonders of the market system embrace all sorts of weird and even mystical explanations as to why slumps occur. In the 19th century one of the founders of 'marginalist economics' Jevons, blamed them on sunspots which, he claimed, affected the weather. The crisis of 1973-75 led to a sudden fashion for theories which claimed the world was running out of oil and even facing a new ice age. The crisis of the early 1990s has led to even

41

stranger conclusions, like those of William Huston, who, according to the *Financial Times*, is 'one of the world's most respected cycle analysts'. He holds that 'cosmic cycles'—for instance the relative positions of the planets Jupiter and Saturn in relation to Earth—can directly cause economic catastrophes. Meanwhile, Sir Roy Calne, professor of surgery at Cambridge University, believes there are simply too many people in the advanced industrial countries to 'support full employment' and that the only answer to this is to limit parenting to those who are over 25 and who can provide proof of 'sufficient maturity and financial resources to take proper care of the child'.

Alongside such lunatic explanations of what goes wrong in a slump are some which contain at least elements of truth. The most common explanation of this kind is the one that blames everything on speculation and speculators. If only this aspect of capitalism could be avoided, it is claimed, then slumps need never happen.

Speculation certainly does play a role. It allows some capitalists to enrich themselves while ignoring the real processes of wealth creation. Speculators make enormous fortunes with each boom by borrowing in order to push up prices and pushing up prices in order to borrow. The result is growing indebtedness which vastly exaggerates the 'hangover effect' when the slump eventually comes. Speculation also increases the difficulties for a capitalist government trying to keep any sort of grip on what is happening to the national economy as billions or even trillions of dollars and yens a day flow from one country to another.

However, speculation and speculators are not the cause of the boom-slump cycle. That lies in the capitalist organisation of production, in the competition between industrial capitalists to make profits. Speculation and speculators serve to intensify booms and slumps which would occur anyway. They are not the main parasites leading the system into crisis, but rather parasites which feed off other parasites.

Some politicians and mainstream commentators claim everything would be alright if only the speculators were eliminated. This has often been the argument of those who want a slightly reformed version of the present capitalist system. In 1964, for instance, the British Labour prime minister, Harold Wilson, claimed it was 'the gnomes of Zurich' who forced him to abandon his election promises when, in fact, it was pressure from the main sections of British big business. Today economic writers like Will Hutton put most of the blame for the crisis on the 'short termism' of the financial institutions of the City of London, virtually ignoring the role played by the big industrialists. And on the far right, fascists and Nazis have always found it easy to rant about 'financiers'— claiming they are 'alien', 'cosmopolitan' or 'Jewish'—as a way of diverting people's anger away from the big industrial capitalists. In fact, industrial capitalists and financial capitalists are rarely two entirely different groups of people. Industrial capitalists will seek to boost their profits through speculation whenever this seems an easy option—for instance gambling on foreign exchange markets—while financial capitalists often seek to enhance their own fortunes by buying up industrial companies.

One final point. People sometimes confuse slumps with the 'collapse' of the capitalist system, or at least claim there can never be any recovery from the slump.

But even in the deepest slump, not all capitalists go bust. There will always be some who see ways of making profits out of other people's poverty—from opening pawn shops and hawking food that's past its sell by date to setting up as company liquidators or providing security guards to protect the rich from the poor. And so the system can survive even the worst crash unless successful workers' struggle replaces it with a better form of society.

This means that, although crises do not end automatically and smoothly as supporters of the system claim, a point is eventually reached at which some capitalists are confident enough of profits to begin investing again. In fact, the slump itself makes it possible for some capitalists to increase their profitability and their output by buying up on the cheap the raw materials and machinery of firms that have gone bust. It usually exerts some downward pressure on labour costs as workers, terrified of losing their jobs, accept worse pay and conditions. And once the slump has been going for a time, rising interest rates are usually followed by falling ones, enabling capitalists to borrow more easily.

So it is that after a period of months or sometimes years there is some revival of production—a few more workers are taken on. There are then more markets for other firms which can themselves increase production, take on more workers and so on. The vicious downward circle of the slump can give way to the rising, 'virtuous' circle of 'recovery' until a new boom results, and with it a new, shortlived spell of super-optimism among the capitalist class and

43

their intellectual apologists. Once again there is talk of 'miracles' just as the ingredients come together for yet another destructive slump.

CHAPTER 3

Getting worse

12 Worsening crises

The pattern of slump-boom-slump-boom can be seen clearly in the economic statistics for most of the 19th century during which Marx wrote. Periods of rapidly rising output, with unemployment falling to about 2 percent of the workforce, alternated with periods of falling output, with unemployment rising to about 10 percent. The alternation seemed to follow a regular, natural rhythm like that of the moon or of the biblical 'seven good years and seven bad years'. But there was also a long term tendency, over several cycles, for slumps to get deeper and longer and for booms to get shallower and shorter.

So the late 1870s and 1880s—the time from which the Carnegie comment comes—was often referred to as the 'Great Depression', meaning that internationally the capitalist economy seemed in worse trouble than any known before. Nearly 50 years later, the 1930s, with much higher levels of unemployment still, were referred to likewise as the 'Great Depression'.

How is this worsening of capitalist crisis to be accounted for?

Some of the early pro-capitalist economists like David Ricardo had noted that profit rates declined over time. They were much lower when Ricardo and others wrote than they had been ten or 20 or 30 years before. This decline in profit rates could explain the deepening of slumps, since with lower average profit rates it would take longer for industry to recover after each down turn.

But how was the decline in profit rates itself to be explained?

Ricardo explained this by a phenomenon to be found in agriculture—the 'law of diminishing returns'. Beyond a certain point, the output of crops from a certain field does not grow as quickly as the amount of seeds you plant or the effort you put into irrigating them, because you begin to approach the limits of the soil's fertility. The trouble with this theory, which is still taught in 'neoclassical' economics today, is that there is no obvious reason why it should apply to the production of manufactured goods. Often it is relatively cheaper to manufacture things in long production runs, not shorter ones. But if that is so, there is no reason why the rate of profit should fall.

Consequently, the deepening of crises and the rising level of unemployment is a complete mystery to modern day capitalist economists. As one of them, Andrew Oswald of the London School of Economics, says:

> Rising unemployment across the nations of the western world looks unstoppable... The truth is economists do not know why unemployment has been tending upwards.

Marx, however, had an explanation for the falling rate of profit—and therefore for the long term deepening of crises and growing levels of unemployment.

He said it was built into the very nature of capitalist accumulation. Each capitalist is in competition with every other capitalist. The only way to survive in this competition is to introduce ever new machines, embodying ever greater amounts of 'dead labour'.

Each capitalist has to introduce as much labour saving equipment as possible. And so investment grows faster than labour force.

You can see this today if you look at the investments of virtually any firm. It is invariably accompanied by 'rationalisation'—by reducing the number of workers required for each task. This does not always mean that the total workforce falls. Sometimes a massive increase in output allows the total workforce to grow. But it very rarely keeps up with the growth in total output or the expansion of total investment.

The ratio of investment to labour (which Marx referred to as 'the organic composition of capital') tends to rise.

There are many empirical studies which show this happening over the last quarter of a century. The American economist

N M Bailey showed in the reputable *Bookings Papers* in 1981 that the ratio of capital to labour in US manufacturing was 1.43 in 1957-68 and 2.24 in 1972-75, while the Oxford statistician Colin Clark showed a rise in the ratio of capital to output in Britain from 1.78 in 1959-62 to 2.19 in 1972-75. The *Financial Times* columnist Samuel Brittan noted with bewilderment in 1977:

> There has been an underlying long term decline in the amount of output per unit of capital in manufacturing…in the industrial countries… One can construct a fairly plausible story for any one country, but not for the industrial world as a whole.

An article in Lloyd's Bank *Economic Review* (June 1989) tells how: 'In the UK, as in many modern industrial countries, the working population tends to be static, while the stock of capital grows…'

The growth in the ratio of investment to labour is not a problem for the individual firm. All a particular firm is concerned with is getting labour saving equipment more quickly than its competitors so as to be able to produce more cheaply and undercut them. So the individual firm will always tend to go for the latest machinery using the smallest amount of labour, knowing this will enable it to grab markets from its rivals and raise its profits at their expense.

But it can become a problem for capitalism as a whole. For if every firm is introducing labour saving equipment, then the ratio of investment to labour throughout the whole system will grow greater.

As we have seen, it is labour, not machinery, that creates value. When machinery grows faster than labour, investment grows faster than value. And, if the proportion of value going to the employers as surplus value is fixed, then investment grows faster than surplus value—or, as we would put it in everyday language, investment rises much faster than profit.

But if this is so, then the rate of profit—the ratio of profit to investment—must decline.

In other words, the greater the success of capitalists in accumulating, the greater is the pressure throughout the system for the rate of profit to fall.

It is important to notice that this whole argument rests on seeing how what is good for the individual capitalist is bad for the capitalist system as a whole. The individual capitalist invests because with more advanced labour saving technology he can beat his competitors and grab some of the profit that previously went to them. But if all capitalists do this, the total rate of profit falls until it hits all of them. This in turn increases the competitive pressure on each and encourages further investment in labour saving technology and a further fall in profit rates throughout the system.

Some economists claim Marx must be wrong about the falling rate of profit, because no capitalist will ever invest if it reduces his profits. This was the argument advanced by the Japanese economist Okishio and accepted by many would be left wing critics of Marxism, like Ian Steedman, in the 1970s and 1980s. But it is fallacious because it does not see that the individual capitalist can do things to increase his own profit while at the same time acting, inadvertently, to reduce the profitability of the system as whole.

Socialists who accepted the arguments of Okishio and Steedman ended up in the strange situation in the 1970s and 1980s of saying there is no inbuilt downward pressure on profit rates and no reason for slumps to get more intractable. Yet these were years in which profit rates did fall below those known in previous decades and in which three great crises shook the system internationally.

13 Increasing exploitation

The tendency for profit rates to fall does not mean they always do so, any more than the law of gravity prevents some objects (rockets, aircraft) from going upwards. Rather it acts as downward pressure on profit which capitalists seek ways of counteracting.

The most obvious way for them to react to such pressure on profits is to make workers work longer and harder for less pay. Marx described this as the capitalist trying to increase the 'rate of exploitation'. And he said there were three ways they tried to do this.

(i) *Absolute Surplus Value*
Firstly, the capitalist can make workers toil for longer without raising their pay proportionately. The result is that the number of 'surplus' hours the worker gives to the capitalists

rises 'absolutely'—which is why Marx refers to this as increasing 'absolute surplus value'.

This method of forcing profits up was very widespread in the early days of industrial capitalism, and Marx's *Capital* provides many examples of it. However, for much of the present century it seemed to have passed into history. In the advanced industrial countries, at least, workers' resistance had forced capitalists to concede a shorter working week and holidays with pay. The 72 hour weeks of Victorian times had become the 48 hour week and then the 44 hour week. During the economic crisis of the early 1930s the US Congress even went so far as to vote for a bill which would have reduced the working week to 30 hours. And although this bill was eventually blocked by big business opposition, the received wisdom was that the future would see workers enjoying ever greater amounts of leisure.

As B K Hunnicut says in a study of working hours in the US, there were confident predictions that:

> Hours of work would continue to decline as they had for over a hundred years, and that before this century was over, less than 660 hours per year would be required of the average worker—less than 14 hours a week.

But, 'in reality, the century long movement [for reducing working hours] had reached a turning point in 1933, and the process suddenly reversed, with hours of work getting longer for a decade.'

In the 1940s American working hours stabilised at the new, higher level. But then with a renewed period of economic crisis after 1973 they got longer again, as Hunnicut also says:

> The Louis Harris organisation conducted a series of polls over the last 15 years concerning the average working week in the US. The found that the average working week increased 20 percent, from 40.6 hours in 1973 to 48.4 hours in 1985.

In Britain the average working week today is an hour longer than in 1983, with the average male worker doing 45.1 hours a week including overtime. In Japan the average working year fell until the mid-1970s, but then stabilised. In mainland Western Europe the downward trend in working hours continued to the beginning of the 1990s recession. But since then employers have been exerting increasing pressure to reverse the trend, claiming that such hours make European firms uncompetitive compared with Japan and the US. It required strike action by the German metal workers' union to stop employers reneging on their promise to introduce the 35 hour week.

(ii) 'Relative Surplus Value'

Secondly, the capitalists can pressure the workers into working harder. Marx pointed out that once capitalists found they could not increase the working week any further in the mid-19th century, they turned to imposing on the workers 'increased expenditure of labour in a given time, heightened tension of labour power, and closer filling up of the pores in the working day...'

The drive for increased productivity became an obsession for big business, as was shown by the movement for 'scientific management' founded by the American F W Taylor in the 1890s. Taylor believed that every task done in industry could be broken down into individual components and timed, so as to determine the maximum which workers could accomplish. In this way, any breaks in the tempo of work could be eliminated, with Taylor claiming he could increase the amount of work done in a day by as much as 200 percent.

Taylorism found its fullest expression with the introduction of the assembly line in Henry Ford's car plants. The speed at which people worked now depended on the speed at which the line moved, rather than their individual motivation. In other industries, the same pressure on people to work flat out was achieved by increasing surveillance by supervisors, with, for instance, mechanical counters on machines indicating the level of work achieved. And today a similar approach is being attempted in a variety of white collar occupations with increased use of assessment, attempts at payment by results, the use of keystroke counters on computers, and so on.

Increasing the intensity of work has three advantages for capitalists.

The first capitalist to increase the intensity of his workers' labour is able to produce more in the same time than his rivals and so undercut them in the market. But he loses the advantage once the other capitalists copy him and increase the productivity of their workers. This is why the drive to increase productivity is endless and why workers make a terrible mistake when they accept the capitalist's argument that increased productivity will protect jobs—all that it does is trap workers in different firms in an endless and futile battle to work harder than each other.

The second gain for the capitalists is more permanent. Increased productivity means that workers produce the equivalent to their own livelihood in a shorter time than before. So instead of taking, say, four hours to produce the goods necessary to renew their ability to work (their labour power), they can do so in three or even two hours. If the working day remains the same length, the share of it going to the capitalist as surplus value can increase.

Surplus value grows relative to labour power, even though the total working day remains fixed. For this reason, Marx called this phenomenon increased 'relative surplus value'.

Increasing the intensity of production has a third advantage for capitalists, especially during a time of rapid technological change. It enables them to get more work out of their machinery before it gets out of date. This is particularly valuable to them if they combine increased intensity of labour with shift systems and flexible working that enable them to run the machinery all hours of the day and every day of the week.

So important is increasing the intensity of labour that capitalists have, on occasions, been willing to do a trade off, by which they accept a shorter working day in return for increased productivity. Marx noted:

> Where we have labour, not carried on by fits and starts, but repeated day after day with unvarying uniformity, a point must inevitably be reached where extension of the working day and intensity of labour mutually exclude each other, in such a way that lengthening the working day becomes compatible only with lower intensity, and a higher degree of intensity only with a shortening of the working day.

From the capitalist side Taylor saw this clearly. One of his schemes to drive up the intensity of work applied to a group of women inspection workers. They had a ten and a half hour day, but he noted that they spent some of the time chatting to each other. He cut their working day by a couple of hours while moving their chairs further apart so they could not talk to each other. This increased their output enormously, although it made them so much more tired that their attention to their work fell. Taylor's reaction was then to provide them with four ten minute breaks in which they were encouraged to walk round and talk to each other, so recovering their attentiveness.

51

In a somewhat similar way, Henry Ford tried to insist that as well as working flat out his workers had fixed spells of 'leisure'—and tried to supervise these so as to prevent the workers wasting them on things like alcohol which would sap their working ability.

The same attitudes persist in some companies today. The *Financial Times* management page can report that in Japan: 'Many companies have banned excessive hours... Oki electric, the machinery manufacturer, said that its researchers would be evaluated by their research results rather than the number of hours spent working'. It goes on to report that in Britain too, there is 'concern about over work' as 'many managers realise, for example, that unless employees take holidays and maintain a life outside work they will fail to perform effectively'.

In fact, this talk of conceding a shorter working week in return for increased intensity of labour rarely gets translated into practice these days. In Japan the working year has remained at 2,100 hours for more than a decade, with one male worker in six doing more than 3,100 hours. In Britain managers still prefer to pressurise existing workers into doing longer hours rather than taking on new workers, so that the average manual worker does an average of nine hours overtime a week, while bosses in sectors like further and higher education are doing their utmost to enforce a longer working week and shorter holidays upon employees. In Germany employers, beaten back on their attempt to scupper the 35 hour week agreement, are now doing their best to force acceptance of Sunday working. As Reiner Hoffman, of the European trade union institute, told the *Financial Times*, 'The major concern of European employers is to reduce unit labour costs to a minimum in the interests of competitiveness.' This has meant attempting to force workers to accept more 'flexible' working patterns, with more shift working, more weekend working and more acceptance of 'annualised hours' systems, which compel workers to do a longer working week than usual whenever it suits the employer.

There is a simple reason why the trend today is once more towards a lengthening rather than a reduction in work hours. Marx pointed out in *Capital* that there are limits to the extent to which increasing the intensity of labour can offset pressure on profit rates.

Those pressures arise, it will be recalled, because the total amount of employed labour power throughout the system does not rise as fast as investment—indeed, it can even begin to fall in absolute terms. But, however hard they are forced to work, a small group of workers cannot produce as much surplus value as a big group.

A simple example shows this. Assume there are one million workers each working an eight hour day, with four hours of that being sufficient to repay the employer for the costs of their wages. The capitalist class will get from them the equivalent of four million hours of surplus value a day.

What happens if the workforce is cut to 100,000 as a result of new technology which increases productivity tenfold?

The workers can now cover the cost of their wages in one tenth of four hours—that is in 24 minutes. The employers now get a huge 7 hours 36 minutes of surplus value from each worker. But the total surplus value from the workforce as a whole does not increase. In fact, it falls from 4 x 1 million = 4 million hours, to 100,000 x 7hours 36minutes = 760,000 hours. And even if immense pressure is applied to the workers to make them work twice as hard, the amount of surplus labour each provides will only rise by an additional 12 minutes per worker—or by a mere 12 minutes x 100,000 = 20,000 hours altogether.

In this way, capitalists eventually find there are limits to their ability to compensate for the fall in the rate of profit by increasing the productivity of their workers. And when that happens, they will be enormously tempted to try to lengthen working hours. After all, in our example, every extra hour the workers can be forced to provide without a wage increase adds 100,000 hours to surplus value—or five times as much as making them work twice as hard.

In practice, of course, capitalists are rarely able to make workers do longer hours without giving anything in return. Usually they pay overtime rates. But often they regard these as paying for themselves, since many workers will, mistakenly, put up with low hourly rates provided there is sufficient overtime to enable them to just make ends meet.

(iii) '*Immiseration*'

The third way for capitalists to try to raise their profit levels is crude wage cutting—or, as Marx put it, 'the absolute immiseration of workers'. Because Marx used this phrase, there have been many crude attacks on his economic analysis for allegedly claiming workers can only get poorer under capitalism. This, for instance, is the reason William Keegan, the economic columnist of the *Observer* newspaper, gives for dismissing Marx's ideas in his book *The Spectre of Capitalism*.

But Marx does not claim that wages always go down under capitalism. He lived in England in the third quarter of the 19th century when he could see this certainly was not happening. And he explicitly rejected the 'iron law of wages' of the German socialist leader Lassalle, which held wages could never rise. Instead, Marx argued that capitalists would try to counter the downward pressure on profit rates by cutting back on the share of output that went to wages. When total output was rising, this was quite compatible with a limited increase in workers' living standards. There could be 'relative immiseration' as the workers' share of output fell, without workers themselves getting worse off.

In practice, capitalists are often trying to get workers to increase productivity in exchange for limited improvements in wages. So workers in the major European countries in the 1970s and 1980s saw small improvements in their living standards even during a period of crises. But they paid for these improvements by increased shift working, increased tiredness and increased stress.

Thus a 1978 survey of 26 year old men in Britain reported that 38 percent felt they were under severe nervous strain at work; a 1982 survey revealed that 19 percent of men and 23 percent of women in semi-skilled and unskilled jobs 'experienced emotional strain'; a 1980s study found that 'machine paced' workers 'maintain high levels of adrenalin during off-the-job hours... Workers complained of an inability to unwind and relax after working all day. Additionally they reported being too tired to interact with their spouse and children after working all day'.

The picture seems to be growing worse. Surveys by Swedish trade unions show that the proportion of workers who felt their jobs involved 'a high degree of stress or mental strain' grew from 9 percent in 1970 to 15 percent in 1980, while the numbers reporting stress 'to some extent' rose from 22 percent to 37 percent; most blamed 'the escalated pace of work'. The Swedish Institute for Social Research found 'a steady increase in the proportion of the population having stressful working conditions'. Japanese surveys showed that rather than reducing workloads, 'the increasing use of robots and other microelectronic technology is resulting in more overtime, less leave and greater mental stress at factories and plants'. And in Britain a recent survey of managers by psychologist David Lewis shows that 'office workers are being put under too much stress and moving towards a Japanese style working week of 12-hour days and work filled evenings' as 'office staff work harder than ever, with lunch breaks cut to 20 minutes'.

A point can be reached in which capitalists despair of raising profits sufficiently just by pushing down the workers' share of output and begin to pursue policies of trying to reduce wages absolutely. This has been happening in the US over the last 20 years. Average wages have fallen as employers have forced 'concessions' including wage cuts from unions and have followed a 'runaway shop' strategy of shifting factories from regions with strong unions to regions with weak unions, cutting wages by up to half in the process.

Attempts are now being made to repeat the process in Britain, with 'contracting out' being used to force workers to accept lower wages to keep their jobs in areas like cleaning, catering, sections of the civil service and so on. When such methods no longer work, firms threaten to move production overseas, to countries where workers are less well organised and wages are lower.

The tendency to increase 'absolute surplus value', 'relative surplus value' and 'immiseration' are not 'laws of the capitalist economy' if by that is meant inbuilt trends that cannot be resisted. They are, rather, methods the capitalists turn to once profit rates come under pressure. But they are also methods which invariably incur resistance from workers, leading to an accentuation of bitterness in society and making widespread class struggle more likely.

14 Never nasty enough

Capitalists try to raise the level of exploitation in order to counter the fall in the rate of profit and protect themselves against the crisis.

One of the tenets of the monetarist version of neo-classical economics is that crisis can be avoided if capitalists are successful in doing this. Provided wages fall sufficiently, it holds, a point will be reached at which 'marginal costs of production' fall below prices, profitability will be restored, capitalists will start investing again and the market for goods will grow until there is full

55

employment. The key to solving the crisis, it insists, is breaking 'trade union monopolies' over labour which prevent the fall in wages.

But the whole history of capitalism shows that increasing the rate of exploitation in this way does not ward off slumps. Slumps have occurred just as much in countries where trade unions are weak or non-existent as in countries where they are strong. In the early 1930s the weakness of British and American trade unions—and the virtual non-existence of trade unions in Fascist Italy—did nothing to stop the onset of slump. In the 1980s and 1990s the weakening of unions in Britain and the US under Thatcher and Reagan did not prevent recession being much deeper than in the 1940s, 1950s and 1960s when unions were much stronger.

One of the powerful points made by the Keynesian economists of the 1930s and 1940s against the old orthodoxy was that cutting wages could actually deepen the crisis, not end it.

Unemployment grows with the onset of slump because firms cannot sell the goods they produce. Cutting wages reduces the total market for consumer goods and therefore means fewer goods can be sold. The immediate effect, then, of wage cutting—or of increasing productivity without increasing wages—is to widen the gap between what is produced and what can be bought. It is to *deepen* the slump.

Of course, this would not matter if investment were to rise automatically to compensate for any decrease in consumption due to wage cutting. The demand for new industrial building and machines would make up for the drop in the demand for consumer goods. But there is no mechanism which ensures that a fall in consumption is automatically balanced by a rise in investment. Indeed, if firms expect consumption to fall, they are likely to fear that the market for their goods will contract and to reduce their investment to avoid ending up with factories capable of producing many more goods than they can sell.

The orthodox neo-classical economists have never been able to answer the Keynesians' devastating critique of their position. All they have ever done is to assert that, if slumps do not solve themselves, it is because workers' resistance to falling wages has not been broken enough.

But there was also always a weakness in the Keynesian case— a weakness which is also found in some Marxists influenced by

Keynesianism, like the Americans Paul Baran and Paul Sweezy. They could not explain why investment should remain so low as to lead to deeper slumps and smaller booms. This is because the Keynesians accepted much of the orthodox 'neo-classical' economics and so could not see that there was bound to be a long term downward pressure on profits which could not be stopped by wage cutting. Keynes himself had spoken of a fall in what he called 'the marginal efficiency of capital' and had expected this to continue in future. Most of his followers abandoned this notion and based themselves on passages in his writings which blamed the crisis on the psychological condition of businessmen rather on some innate tendency in the capitalist system. If firms undertook investment, these passages claimed, it was because of 'animal spirits—of a spontaneous urge for action rather than inaction'. But, 'if the animal spirits are dimmed and the spontaneous optimism falters…enterprise will fade and die' so that 'slumps and depressions are exaggerated in degree'.

The Keynesians therefore argued that the tendency towards slumps could be stopped by limited government intervention in the economy designed to create a feeling of optimism about future prospects among those who ran big business. In a slump, they argued, the government should spend money and discourage wage cutting. In this way, it would create a market for goods, allow firms to expand their output and encourage investment by making it seem likely that markets would grow still further. The increased wealth created as the economy recovered from slump would, they further argued, allow a rise in both working class incomes and profits.

Keynesian ideas dominated mainstream economic thinking in the quarter of a century after the 1930s slump, as we have seen earlier. But they lost their influence with the crisis of the mid-1970s. A high degree of government intervention in all the major economies failed to stop that crisis and the only result seemed to be to superimpose a high level of inflation on the rising levels of unemployment. Almost everywhere governments and businessmen retreated into the old orthodoxy which held that the answer to slumps lay in combining anti-union laws with rising unemployment to hold wages down.

Economists influenced by Keynesianism, like Galbraith in the US and William Keegan, Will Hutton and Paul Ormerod in Britain, have been able to punch enormous holes through this reborn old

57

orthodoxy. Yet they cannot themselves point to any sure way of ending the increasingly severe slumps. Their own remedy to low investment consists in urging Britain and America to copy the methods of the German and Japanese economies—although these economies have been going through severe slumps of their own. And they want the same holding down of wages as do the monetarists, except they want the government to have incomes policies rather than simply leaving things to the market to impoverish workers.

But on one thing Keynes certainly was right. Holding down consumption increases the likely impact of any crisis. For it means there is a growing disproportion between the potential output of the economy and the consumption levels of the mass of the people. Investment has to fill an even bigger gap if all the goods produced are going to be sold. The likelihood of a situation arising in which they cannot be sold, in which there is 'overproduction', grows greater.

If profit rates are not high enough to bring that investment about, then a deep slump occurs. Capitalists find themselves in a Catch 22 situation. If they increase exploitation in order to raise profits, then the gap to be filled is still greater. If they reduce exploitation in order to expand the market for consumer goods, profit rates fall and investment is not high enough to stop a slump developing anyway.

The dilemma arises because accumulation has proceeded to such a level that there is a huge contrast between the scale of production and the size of the workforce. This finds expression through the workforce not being able to produce enough profit to match the level of investment needed, leading to capitalists refusing to invest and to firms being unable to sell all their produce.

In a sane society there would be no such dilemma. For there is an absolute need for the goods produced, if society's priorities were the well-being of the mass of people. But the motive force of the present system is not people's well-being. Those who control capital behave the way they do in order to increase their profits, to expand their holding of capital. Precisely because of this, huge sectors of the productive apparatus of capitalism grind to a halt.

Worsening crises are not a result of human frailty or some natural catastrophe. They are, rather, an inbuilt fault of a system in which the satisfaction of human need through productive labour is subordinated to the drive of capitalists to accumulate ever more wealth in their own hands. They show, in Marx's words, that 'the capitalist mode of production meets in the development of the productive forces a barrier which has nothing to do with the production of wealth as such', that 'the real barrier of capitalist production is capital itself'.

This is why deepening crises cause such perplexity to pro-capitalist economists of all sorts. Even those economists and politicians who want to reform the system take its basic features for granted. And so they end up seeing growing unemployment, deepening pools of poverty, the 'end of lifetime employment', growing insecurity and ever greater pressures to work harder as natural phenomena like earthquakes or tempests, which we cannot prevent and have to learn to live with.

15 How the system keeps going

Conventional economics assume that capitalism will go on for-ever, with crisis as an accident that occurs sometimes. Marx's analysis, by contrast, shows that worsening slumps are endemic in the system. But that does not mean capitalism simply collapses of its own accord, or that slumps go on forever. In the century and a quarter since Marx finished *Capital* the system has known booms—some going on for a very long period of time—as well as slumps, and there have been periods in which workers' living standards have improved, as well as periods in which they have got worse.

What is more, the system as a whole has expanded massively over the long term. When Marx started his researches in the 1840s, industrial capitalism was characteristic only of the north of England, parts of Belgium and the north eastern seaboard of the United States, along with small patches of France and Germany. By the time he died in the 1880s, it was dominant right across north western Europe and throughout North America, and was making its first advances in Japan. Today, every country on the globe is dominated by it. Today, total output of the world's economy is four or five times what it was in 1945, and 20 or 30 times what it was in the 1840s.

If Marx's account of capitalism had simply talked about the capitalist system stagnating or declining, it would clearly have been just as mistaken as those orthodox economic schools that only talk about the expansion of the system.

In fact, Marx insisted that alongside the tendency for the rate of profit to fall there exist certain 'countervailing factors'.

What were these countervailing factors? Some we have already looked at—the various measures capitalists take to raise the rate of exploitation and so push up profit rates. But in themselves these cannot stop crises. Neither can they halt the long term trend for profit rates to decline, since, as we have also seen, a few workers exploited intensively cannot produce as much surplus value as a much larger group of workers less intensively exploited.

Another factor that helped raise profit rates in Marx's own day was foreign trade. At that time the fully capitalist economies were surrounded by much larger pre-capitalist societies in Asia, Africa, Latin America and Eastern Europe. The capitalists could use the crudest means (pillaging India, moving millions of slaves from Africa to the Americas, compelling the Chinese to buy opium, conquering Egypt at the behest of the bankers) to get hold of the wealth of these societies at below its real value and so raise their own profits.

This is not a method that can work for any length of time today, now that the whole world is capitalist. The capitalists of one country can improve their position by forcing the rulers of other countries to sell them goods cheaply—as with Middle East oil in the 1960s and early 1970s. But this entails the redistribution of profits between capitalist countries, not the raising of profits right across the capitalist world.

For Marx a third 'countervailing' factor was vitally important, and remains so today. This is the way in which each individual crisis has an impact on the long term trends within the system.

Crises are devastating for capitalism. They create panic within ruling classes and misery among the mass of the people. But they also have advantages for those individual capitalists who manage to avoid going bust. For they find they can buy up the assets of other capitalists on the cheap and can use the high levels of unemployment to force down wages.

Thus during the great Wall Street crash of 1929 some capitalists were able to sit back and wait until stock prices were at record lows and then move in to buy up whole companies on the cheap. In the more recent slump of the early 1990s the Canary Wharf office development in London's East End which had cost £2 billion to build was reduced in value to £60 million. This was devastating to its original owners, the Reichman Brothers, who were forced out of business. But it was a godsend to the firms which bought it up at a bargain basement price.

Capitalist firms survive the slump by cannibalism, by some eating up others. The survivors can get hold of means of production at a price much lower than their old value. They find they can begin to expand production using the most modern plant and machinery without paying the full price for it. Investment can grow in extent without growing in cost. This prevents the cost of investment growing much more quickly than the total labour force— easing the pressure on the rate of profit.

The crisis forces a 'restructuring' of capitalism, in which many individual firms go to the wall, allowing the survivors to recover their profits at the expense of others. And because so much capital is 'written off' during the slump, the long term growth of investment compared with the labour force is not nearly as marked as it would be otherwise. So recession has the paradoxical effect of allowing profit rates and industrial expansion to recover.

As one history of modern economic crises notes, when the US went rapidly into recession in 1884, 'failures came in quick succession; unemployment increased and wages fell 25 to 30 percent in textiles and by 15 to 22 percent in the iron and steel industry…' But the Carnegie group for one had saved up large profits during the previous boom and was 'thus able during the depression to buy up competing factories cheaply. There was a general improvement in the economic climate in early 1886…'

In a similar way, recovery from the recession in Britain in the early 1890s was associated with a wave of takeovers by five big banks (Barclays, Lloyds, Midland, National Provincial and Westminster) which gave them a virtual monopoly. Alongside this there was a concentration of ownership in textiles and metallurgy, widespread rationalisation of industry, the introduction of new technologies in the shoe making and printing industries, and several great lockouts which forced workers to accept lower wages and a worsening of conditions.

Crises blunted the tendency for investment to rise much more quickly than the labour force through the second half of the 19th century. But they did not do away with this tendency completely. According to one estimate the ratio of investment to labour in the

US doubled between 1880 and 1912, according to another it rose by 25 percent between 1900 and 1918, while a third estimate suggests the ratio of investment to output rose from 2.02 in 1855-64 to 2.16 in 1875-83.

As an important study by Gillman has noted, the ratio of investment to labour in the US 'displays a fairly persistent tendency to rise' in the period, although 'it was fairly slow compared with Marx's hypothetical example'. The result was that by the end of the century, as historian Eric Hobsbawm has noted:

> Both the old and the new industrial economies ran into problems of markets and profit margins... As the titanic profits of the industrial pioneers declined, businessmen searched desperately for a way out.

A similar pattern was to be seen in Britain in the 1980s. The recession of 1980-82 led to something like a third of manufacturing capacity shutting down, even though firms were producing about the same amount as before by 1987. This slowed down considerably the growth of investment compared with labour. As the article in *Lloyds Bank Review* quoted earlier told:

> The capital stock has been rising, but at a declining rate. It was rising at 4 percent in 1970, decelerating to 2 percent by 1982...

Under these conditions, increasing exploitation of workers—who accepted small wage cuts and more onerous working conditions out of fear of unemployment—could actually raise the rate of profit a little. But again, as a century earlier, the recovery of profit rates was only a partial recovery, above the level of the early 1980s, but still substantially below that for the 1950s, 1960s and early 1970s. This was brought home in a devastating fashion when boom suddenly gave way to slump, first in Britain and the US, then in France, Germany and Japan, in the early 1990s.

CHAPTER 4

Getting bigger

16 The concentration of capital

The way in which recession can ease some of the long term problems of capitalism has led some supporters of the system to claim there are no such long term problems. People like former Tory chancellor of the exchequer Nigel Lawson say that recurrent crises are nothing to worry about, since slumps are invariably followed by booms. The Austrian school of economists including Hayek positively revel in the 'destruction' of the slump since, they say, it is 'creative', laying the ground for the production of ever greater amounts of wealth.

A variant of this argument is to be found among some people influenced by Marxism. The restructuring of the system and the 'devaluation' of capital that occurs in a recession, they say, allows the system to purge itself of all the downward pressures on the rate of profit. As a result, there need be no long term tendency for slumps to get worse or booms to be shallower and shorter. The alternation of boom and slump may have horrible effects for workers, they imply, but there is no reason why the system cannot go on as it is at present indefinitely. Nor, they sometimes add, is there any reason why a Labour type government should not be able to improve the condition of workers within the system.

But any such argument ignores something else that happens to capitalism as it gets older. The number of competing firms tends

63

to get fewer, while a handful of very large firms come to dominate whole industries and whole economies—a process which Marx called the 'concentration and centralisation of capital'.

If any one of these giant firms goes bust, there is enormous damage to the rest of the economy. Banks that have lent it money are very badly hit. So too are other industrial firms which expected to sell it machinery and raw materials or to sell consumer goods to its workers. Suddenly their profits are turned into losses. Such is the scale of the damage that the ability of other firms to buy up machinery and raw material on the cheap does not nearly begin to compensate for it. Instead of the destruction of some firms benefiting others, what threatens to develop is an economic black hole that sucks into it profitable and unprofitable firms alike.

The result is that, once the system is dominated by a handful of giant firms, crises do not automatically resolve themselves. Instead they get worse as each giant that collapses knocks over others in a domino effect.

Many apologists for capitalism try to deny that there is a tendency for the system to be dominated by a handful of big firms in this way. So Thatcherites in Britain, Republicans in the US, even Islamists in Algeria talk of the importance of small or medium size firms, claiming these are the dynamic centre of the economy. But this ignores the way that each crisis leads to some firms eating up others, concentrating capital in fewer hands. Of course, new firms do arise as individuals find, by luck, judgement or crookery, that they are in a situation to set themselves up as capitalists. And, as Marx noted, these new firms, in their eagerness to break into the big time, sometimes show themselves to be much more innovative and competitive than their larger rivals. So, for instance, in the 1970s and 1980s many advances in computing, especially as regards software, were made by medium and small companies. But the great majority of these firms did not survive very long and were soon taken over by giants—either pre-existing ones or new ones. By the 1990s three or four giant firms dominated the field internationally. More generally, the *Financial Times* could report in the autumn of 1992 that, 'a new generation of entrepreneurs that prospered in the boom of the 1980s is systematically being wiped out.'

The result of such a wiping out of small firms in recession after recession for a century and a half has been the increasing dominance of the giants. As Hobsbawm says, already a century ago:

The formation of trusts and cartels characterised Germany and the US in the 1880s... By 1897 there were 82 industrial combinations with a capitalisation of more than 1,000 million dollars, in the three years 1898-1900 eleven great combinations were formed with a capitalisation of 1,140 million dollars, and the greatest combination of all, US Steel, appeared in 1901 with a capitalisation of 1,400 million dollars.

The process was further accelerated during the inter-war years, when in each country a handful of firms came to dominate each industry—for example, Ford, General Motors and Chrysler in the US motor industry, ICI in the British chemical industry, or Krupps and Thyssen in German heavy industry. By the 1970s the degree of economic concentration was such that in the US the hundred biggest firms owned 48.4 percent of industrial assets and in most industries there were two or at the most three major competitors. In Britain at the same time the 100 largest firms produced 49 percent of total output and in many industries, like chemicals, food processing, detergents, mainframe computers and car components, there were at most two competitors.

The recessions of the last 20 years have resulted in still further concentration, with a series of takeovers and alliances between firms that cross national boundaries, so that a firm trading under a US name may well be owned in Britain or France, and one trading under a British name owned in Japan. This is especially true of finance and of the major industries—telecommunications, computers, aerospace, motors, chemicals, food processing, pharmaceuticals—but it is also increasingly true of banking and of a vast range of 'service' industries, from private security to film production.

Today estimates suggest that the 500 biggest transnational corporations control two thirds of world trade, with the 15 biggest—including companies like General Motors, Exxon, IBM and Royal Dutch Shell— having a combined income greater than that of over 120 countries.

If any of these giants goes bust, far from helping to 'clear out' the system it makes problems worse. The result is that, despite what governments say about the wonders of the 'free market', they panic when the market threatens the future of any giants, and do everything they can to keep these corporations afloat.

This was already shown a century ago, when British authorities committed to the market and 'free trade' rushed to prop up

Barings Bank the first time it was on the verge of collapse. It was shown on a wider scale in the inter-war years, when in one country after another right wing governments intervened, nationalising firms if necessary, to stop the collapse of major banks and major industries. It was shown again in the 1980s, when the Bush government in the US intervened to bail out the Savings and Loan institutions and the Thatcher government organised a 'lifeboat' operation to salvage the Johnson Matthey Bank.

There were more outright bankruptcies in the early 1990s than there were in the recessions of the mid-1970s or the early 1980s—at least, in the US and Britain. The S&Ls may have been propped up, but a number of big firms on both sides of the Atlantic went to the wall—the giant airline Pan Am, the huge international Bank of Credit and Commerce International, the conglomerate Pollypeck, the property giant Olympia and York, the world's biggest printing concern, Maxwell Communications Corporation.

However, that is not the end of the matter. Even outright bankruptcy did not have the positive impact on the rest of the system it once had. For most of the capital of such giants is not owned by individual shareholders who bear the losses of such collapses and leave other big firms to gain. Instead the main shareholders are banks and other financial institutions and they must seek to recoup their losses from the remaining, profitable sections of the system. So it was the banks who had to pay much of the cost for the collapse of Maxwell, Olympia and York, Pan Am, Pollypeck and so on. In the wake of this the banks sought to make up for these losses by raising their interest rates to other borrowers—including other big firms.

When individual shareholders (or, in the Maxwell case, individual pensioners) suffer, this is advantageous to the system as a whole, enabling it to prosper as the shareholders and their capital are written off. But when the giant financial institutions suffer, the situation is very different. The losses incurred have to be borne by these institutions and so serve to reduce profitability through the rest of the system. This intensifies rather than alleviates its tendency towards crisis.

The clearest sign of this was the continuing high level of long term interest rates right through the recession—generally twice as high as in the 1960s and in marked contrast to what happened in the recession of the early 1980s, when real interest rates were negative.

Instead of clearing room for the rest of the system to resume profitable growth, the bankruptcies of modern day multinationals put a bigger burden on it.

17 Imperialism and war

Capitalism's long term problems were already visible more than a century ago during the 'Great Depression' of the 1880s, when Carnegie complained about the intractability of crises. They were visible again during the 1930s, when some commentators spoke of capitalism's 'final crisis'. In both cases capitalists and workers alike found themselves waiting for a recovery that it seemed would never come.

Yet not only did capitalism recover on both occasions, but the post-depression years were some of the most dynamic in the history of the system. This was especially true of the expansion which took place from the 1940s to the early 1970s. The period saw a 'long boom' that involved the biggest and most sustained spell of expansion in the history of the system.

These experiences led people both at the turn of the century and again in the 1960s to claim that capitalism was gradually giving way to a better form of society, which was not on the verge of collapse, which did not need to experience periodic slumps, and which did not lead to ever more bitter class confrontations.

In fact, on both occasions capitalism discovered new mechanisms for offsetting the tendency of crises to get deeper. But these were temporary measures, and as their effects wore off, crises returned with a vengeance.

The main mechanism at the end of the last century was for capitalism to reach out beyond its original heartlands in Western Europe and North America—a process which became known as imperialism.

In the 1870s and 1880s the major capitalist powers set about expanding and consolidating their hold on much of the rest of the world. British governments extended the old British Empire, to take in about a third of the earth's surface—including half of Africa, the whole Indian subcontinent and much of the Middle East. French governments seized Indochina and most of the rest of Africa, and began to dominate the Lebanon (although it was still allegedly under Turkish control). The United States seized the Philippines from Spain and took control of the nominally

67

independent states of Cuba and central America. Holland spread out from its base in Java to take over all of what is now Indonesia. Belgium took the Congo (now Zaire). Italy seized Tripoli (now Libya) and Somalia. Germany began to dream of a colonial empire of its own, colonising Tanganyka (now Tanzania) and South West Africa (now Namibia), and trying to establish a base in North Africa. All the major European powers established zones of influence in China, effectively dividing the country between them. By 1914 the only country in Africa to remain independent was Ethiopia, while in Asia, apart from divided China, only Afghanistan and Thailand were not ruled directly from Europe.

The European powers carved out these empires because their financiers and industrialists believed there were vast profits to be made there. They saw control of territory as the key to getting cheap raw materials and so gaining an advantage over other capitalist countries.

International diplomacy came to centre on the struggle between the great powers to establish colonies in Africa and Asia and to exercise influence over nominally independent governments in the Middle East, Latin America and Eastern Europe. Those powers with empires sought to strengthen them by building up their military forces. Those without empires sought to take colonies and influence from those with. And, when it came to the crunch, they were prepared to wage world war against each other with Britain, France and Russia on the one side, and Germany and Austro-Hungary on the other.

Some mainstream historians claim the drive to empire was motivated by non-economic considerations. But this ignores the fact that from the 1880s onwards amongst the most enthusiastic supporters of colonisation were the very industrialists and financiers who had been doubtful about its value earlier. By the 1890s half of British total investment was going overseas. Firms whose business depended on empire came to dominate the economies of Britain (with banks like Barings, industrial conglomerates like Unilever, and, increasingly oil companies like Anglo Iranian—now BP—and Shell), France (the Suez Canal company) and Belgium (the giant Union Miniere). In Germany heavy industry applied increasing pressure for the government to carve out a 'sphere of influence' in the Balkans and the remnants of the Turkish empire.

As Eric Hobsbawm has quite rightly noted:

Political historians have professed to find no economic reasons for the virtual division of the world between a handful of West European powers (plus the USA) in the last decades of the nineteenth century. Economic historians have no such difficulty.

Overseas investment took place because industrialists and financiers sought secure profits and cheap raw materials. But it had a very important indirect impact on the system as a whole. If half of investment went overseas, there was a 50 percent reduction in the funds available for investment at home. Firms became less worried that if they did not undertake labour saving investment their domestic competitors would. So overall investment no longer rose faster than the employed labour force: indeed, the ratio of investment to output in Britain actually fell from 2.16 in 1875-83 to 1.82 in 1891-1901. Profit rates were able to rise and the long drawn out capitalist pessimism of the 1880s gave way to a new period of optimism and boom.

Unemployment which had risen to over 13 to 14 percent three times in the years of the 'Great Depression' was less than 10 percent from 1895 to 1912.

No wonder the dominant ideas in the newly founded Labour Party in Britain were 'gradualist'. No wonder too that 'revisionist' and 'gradualist' ideas were increasingly influential in the supposedly 'Marxist' German social democratic party. For a time it did seem to superficial observers that capitalism could provide security and improved living standards for workers.

But the period of capitalist 'prosperity' did not last long. Imperialism was only able to counter falling profitability for a couple of decades. Opportunities for investment overseas eventually began to run out, and profits made on existing investments started to flow back into the advanced capitalist countries. By the end of the first decade of the present century this was raising the level of funds seeking profits in Britain back to that of 20 years before: the ratio of investment to labour in industry rose, according to one calculation, from 1.92 in 1891-92 to 2.19 in 1908-13—that is, to a slightly higher level than on the eve of the 'Great Depression' of the late 1870s and early 1880s. Not surprisingly, there were new signs of downward pressure on profit rates and the crises got more serious, with unemployment rising back to about 15 percent by 1913-14.

At the same time, the pressure for capitalist states with small empires to get a share of the action led to repeated clashes with established imperialisms. The result was a war between the US and Spain over the Philippines and Cuba, a war between Japan and Russia over the domination of North China and Korea in 1904-05, a clash between France and Germany over influence in Morocco, a race between Britain and Germany to build more battleships and, finally, a clash between Russia and Austro-Hungary over influence in south eastern Europe—the clash which precipitated the First World War.

Imperialism had eased the system's tendency to ever greater economic crises, but only for a period, and at the price of leading it to the horror and waste of world war. And in the aftermath of the war, economic crisis re-emerged on a greater and more damaging scale than ever before in the history of the system.

18 Militarism and state capitalism

The crisis that began in 1929 was by far the worst the system had ever known, with unemployment in the two biggest industrial powers, the US and Germany, rising to about a third of the workforce. What is more, the slump showed little sign of ending on its own accord.

It required government intervention to begin bringing about limited economic recovery in both economies in 1933-34, with the Roosevelt 'New Deal' in the US and public works schemes from the new Nazi government in Germany. But neither did more than scratch the surface of the slump. Industrial output in Germany was still only four fifths of the 1929 figure in 1934, while in the US one in seven of the population were still unemployed in 1937 when a new phase of economic downturn started—described by one historian as 'the steepest economic decline in the history of the US'.

Real recovery from the crisis did not start until governments began massive preparations for war. In Germany this happened in 1935 with the establishment of a 'preparedness' economy, based on massive rearmament. It did not happen in the US until 1941 when the country entered the Second World War. As J K Galbraith pointed out: 'The Great Depression of the 1930s never came to an end. It merely disappeared in the great mobilisation of the 1940s.'

Preparation for war had some of the same benefits for capitalism as imperialism, of which it was a logical extension. It offered giant firms the opportunity to seize control of raw materials and industrial plant from their rivals in other countries—as when German big business took over the economies of Czechoslovakia and Poland and began to challenge British big business for control of the Middle East's oil with the 'desert war' in North Africa, or when Japanese big business seized plantations previously run by British, French and Dutch companies in Vietnam, Indonesia and Malaya.

What is more, preparation for war provided firms with a state guaranteed market for their goods which was not affected by fluctuations in the rest of the economy. The demand for food and consumer goods went up and down with boom and slump. So did the demand for factories to make these things and ships and trucks to move them. But the demand for tanks, battleships and military aircraft rose so long as governments continued to arm themselves.

In fact, the state did not merely order arms from the private sector. It increasingly planned the whole economy—if necessary nationalising private firms—in order to make sure arms were produced on time and in the right quantities.

In Nazi Germany from 1935 onwards the state took control of much of the banking system in order to ensure that their deposits were used to finance the arms drive. Industrial concerns were compelled by law to deposit all profits above a certain level with the state for the same purpose. Under the four year plan of 1936 Goering was made 'economic dictator'. His aim was to push through an investment programme of six to eight billion marks, whether it was profitable or not, using every method—investment subsidies, tax exemptions, guarantees of prices, orders and profits. When the head of one giant firm, Thyssen, refused to do what he was told, Goering confiscated his property and forced him to flee into exile.

Similarly, once the US had entered the war, the state controlled not only the armaments sector of the economy—which represented about half the total national output—but also decided what consumer goods should be produced. It became responsible for 90 percent of total investment and spent vast sums building new armaments factories which it then handed over to private firms to run.

71

Effectively, the drive to war led the state to override the old market mechanisms—and to neutralise any opposition to it doing so from the big firms. Economic development inside Nazi Germany or wartime America was no longer dependent on the 'free' flow of funds to the most profitable parts of the economy. Instead the state decided what needed to be produced and then caused funds to flow to the appropriate sectors—whether by giving direct orders to firms or by rigging the market so as to make those sectors profitable.

But it was not only the state's overriding of market mechanisms that made the war economy work. The sheer waste of producing arms and the barbarous destructiveness of war played their part. They had the same impact on the system as the destruction of capital that takes place during a slump has. They reduced the resources available for investment in productive industry—and with that the tendency for investment to grow faster than the labour force.

This was first noted by the German Marxist Grossman writing in the 1920s:

> The destructions and devaluations of war are a means of warding off the immanent collapse [of capitalism], of creating a breathing space for the accumulation of capital... War and the destruction of capital values bound up with it weaken the breakdown [of capitalism] and necessarily provide a new impetus to the accumulation of capital.

Although wars allow some of the biggest individual capitalists to expand their holding massively, the effect on the system as a whole he explained, is to 'pulverise values' and 'slow down accumulation', so that investment does not rise any faster than the employed labour force. That in turn stops the rate of profit falling.

The same argument was developed and expanded in the 1940s, 1950s and 1960s by an American Marxist who wrote under the names Oakes and Vance, and by the British Marxist Mike Kidron. They showed that although arms production slowed down the pace at which capital accumulation occurred, it also allowed it to proceed more smoothly, without coming to a standstill in repeated slumps. The war economy compared to the peace economy was rather like the tortoise compared to the hare in Aesop's fable. At first accumulation in a war economy proceeds more slowly than in a peace economy, because so many resources that could be invested productively are wasted on arms instead. But the war economy, for this very reason, is not forced to stop to 'recover its breath' through a slump, and so overtakes the peace economy.

This was shown dramatically during the Second World War. Of the output of the American economy in 1943, nearly half went on war programmes. Yet, even with this waste, the output of consumer goods was greater than it had been in the slump-becalmed peace economy of the late 1930s. And even after being taxed to pay for some of these arms, the profits of American companies were more than twice as high in the war years as they had been in 1938.

It was shown again in the Cold War years between the late 1940s and the mid-1970s. Most economic observers had expected the post World War Two world to witness a repeat of the great crisis of the inter-war years. It did not happen because arms expenditures remained at a much higher level than ever before during 'peacetime'. From making up less than 1 percent of American output in the 1930s, they were at around 15 percent in the early 1950s, and even during the 1960s, when they were down to about 8 or 9 percent, were still equal to the total investment in civilian industry.

Capitalism experienced what some have called its 'golden age' between the 1940s and the 1970s. Country after country experienced virtually unprecedented economic growth. The American economy trebled in size, that of Germany grew fivefold, that of France fourfold. Even the miserable, long declining British economy was producing twice as much by the 1970s as in the 1940s.

Capitalism prospered as never before. And life for most workers also got better. Unemployment all but disappeared in most of the advanced industrial countries, falling to about 1 percent in Britain, Germany and Scandinavia. Not only were the great cities rebuilt after the devastation of the war, but new housing estates replaced slums that went back to the 1830s or 1840s. Free health services helped people to live longer and improvements in pensions made many able, for the first time, to look forward to their old age.

Poverty did not disappear. It persisted in 'depressed areas' based on old industries that missed out on the boom. It also afflicted the chronically sick, single parent families and some of the old. But in the advanced countries it was usually hidden poverty. The unemployed no longer hung about on the streets as in the 1930s and beggars were unknown.

The boom was a boom of the advanced industrial countries. But it did not leave the rest of the world untouched. Countries like Italy, Spain, Portugal, South Korea and Singapore began to catch up with, and even in a few cases overtake, old established industrial countries like Britain. Elsewhere, in the large 'third world' countries like India, China, Brazil and Mexico there was rapid growth of pockets of industry, even if the mass of the population continued to live in backbreaking poverty in the countryside or in burgeoning urban slums. The growth enabled even the poor to believe that it was only a question of waiting before things got better.

These long years of boom gave rise to very similar ideas that had developed in the 1890s. Capitalism, it seemed to superficial thinkers, had overcome all its problems. Indeed, some writers went so far as to assert it was not capitalism any more but some higher form of economic organisation.

Yet none of this expansion of the system could have occurred without the horrors of World War Two, the immense waste of the post-war arms economy, and the immense danger to the whole of humanity from the nuclear arms race. The 'glories' of the 'golden age' depended on the barbarity of the nuclear bomb.

19 State capitalism, Stalinism and the Third World

Military state capitalism was not something confined to the advanced Western states. For some 40 years it was very much the model for capitalist development right across the world. Indeed, one of the economies to move first and most thoroughly to state capitalism was that of a relatively backward country, Stalin's Russia, in the late 1920s. This called itself socialist. But by the late 1920s the country was already far from the genuine socialism which had inspired the revolution of 1917. This had aimed at a society where workers consciously determined what happened. But the unleashing of civil war by the old ruling class and military intervention by all the Western powers strangled the revolution. There was unparalleled economic devastation, the closing down of almost all of Russian industry and the effective destruction of the working class that had made the revolution. Without the working class there could be no workers' democracy.

The revolutionaries who had led the revolution had remained in power in the early 1920s. But their rule increasingly depended on a bureaucracy made up of many of the administrators of the old Tsarist empire together with a new layer of full time party functionaries headed by Joseph Stalin. Such bureaucrats preserved some of the language of the revolution, but increasingly ruled on their own behalf, driving the revolutionaries of 1917 out of the ruling party. The face of a suffocated corpse may look like that of a living human; similarly in appearances Russia in 1927 resembled Russia in 1917. But in reality it was fundamentally different.

For a time the new rulers of Russia were happy to leave the land and some sections of industry and commerce in private hands, relying on the support of the privileged owners (known as Nepmen) to oust those like Trotsky who wanted to stick by the principles of 1917. But this policy led to a great economic crisis in 1927-28 just as there were renewed threats of Western intervention. The new rulers then did a great U-turn, adopting their own version of military state capitalism.

They were desperate for some means to defend their control over Russia from foreign threats. The answer, they decided, lay in building up industry at the maximum speed. This alone would enable them to produce tanks, battleships, aircraft and machine guns on the same scale as the Western states. As Stalin said:

> To slacken the pace of industrialisation would mean to lag behind and those who lag behind are beaten... We are fifty to one hundred years behind the advanced countries. We must make good this lag in ten years or they will crush us.

Stalin's logic was the same as that of any small capitalist who faces competitive pressure from a bigger capitalist—to tell his workers to make every conceivable 'sacrifice' in order to catch up with the rival.

The way to 'catch up with the West', for Stalin, was to copy inside Russia all the methods of 'primitive accumulation' used elsewhere. The British industrial revolution had been based on driving the peasants from the land through enclosures and clearances; Stalin smashed peasant control of the land through 'collectivisation' which forced millions to migrate to the cities. British capitalism had accumulated wealth through slavery in the Caribbean and North America; Stalin herded millions of people into the slave camps of the Gulag. Britain had pillaged Ireland, India and Africa; Stalin took away the rights of the non-Russian republics of the USSR and deported whole peoples thousands of miles away from their homes. The British industrial revolution had involved denying workers the most elementary rights and making men, women and children work up to 16 hours a day; Stalin followed suit, abolishing the independence of the unions, shooting down strikers, and cutting real wages by about 50 percent.

The only significant difference between Stalin's methods and those of Western capitalism in its infancy was that, while Western capitalism took hundreds of years to complete its primitive accumulation, Stalin sought to achieve his in a couple of decades. The brutality and barbarism were, therefore, much more concentrated in time.

The Stalinist bureaucracy could not 'catch up' by copying the small scale 'market' capitalism of England during the industrial revolution. Russia could only succeed militarily if its industries were similar in size to those of the West. But there was no time to wait for private firms to grow larger as they gobbled each other up. The state had to intervene to bring about the necessary scale of production.

State capitalist monopolies, not small private firms, were to carry accumulation through. And the state had to coordinate the whole economy, subordinating production of everything else to this accumulation.

Most people saw this as socialist—and many still do. For Stalinism did indeed break the backbone of private capitalism in Russia and later in Eastern Europe, China and so on. But its own methods were very similar to those of the Western war economies. It planned as they planned—so as to hold down the consumption of the masses while building up heavy industry and arms production.

As Michael Kaser, one of the foremost Western writers on the East European economies, notes, the new 'socialist planners' in the region after 1945 often simply took over the methods established during wartime German occupation, 'Many market relations suppressed by the price and quantity controls of 1939-45 never reemerged'.

One of the best known Polish planners, Oskar Lange, noted:

Methods of highly centralised administrative planning and management widely using...coercion are not characteristic features of socialism, but rather a technique of the war economy.

Such a model of state intervention and 'planning' had an appeal to the rulers of many of the world's weaker capitalisms in the 1930s, 1940s, 1950s and 1960s. Mussolini's Italy responded to the crisis of the 1930s by setting up two huge state run firms, IRI and ENI, to build up new industries. In Brazil and Argentina authoritarian governments put state run industries at the head of the economy. The rulers of former colonies like India, Egypt, Syria, Iraq and Algeria looked to massive levels of state owner-ship and five year plans to bring about industrialisation. So too did Kuomintang ruled Taiwan and the military dictatorships of South Korea. Right wing French governments adopted an approach called 'indicative planning', while even Britain briefly drew up a (stillborn) long term plan in 1966.

The motives were everywhere the same as Stalin's had been. The rulers of less competitive capitalist countries needed the state to pool their resources and to protect them from the immediate effects of fluctuations in the world market. Otherwise they would never be able to face up to the industries of their bigger and more competitive rivals.

As a result, for nearly half a century the orthodoxy of capital-ist economics was that there had to be state intervention and that 'planning' was a good thing.

John Maynard Keynes had been the apostle of this approach in the West, Joseph Stalin in Russia. They were very different personalities—one a liberal minded academic and civil servant who made himself a million on the stock exchange, the other a murderous dictator. The supporters of one tended to be in the social democratic and Labour parties, of the other in their bitter rivals, the Stalinist parties. Yet they shared one important idea: they each believed that taking over the existing state and using it to direct the national economy could prevent crises and ensure continual industrial advance.

20 The end of an illusion

There were, as we have seen, enormous changes in the fortunes of the capitalist system in the 30 years between 1932 and 1962.

In 1932 all of the predictions Marx had made about the system seemed to be being fulfilled. There was a catastrophic crisis worse than ever before. A third of people were jobless in the world's two largest industrial economies—Germany and US. Millions of middle class people found themselves in the same desperate plight as the mass of workers, even in the advanced economies. In colonial countries the collapse of raw material prices plunged unprecedented numbers into dire poverty. The sheer depth of the crisis was breeding the most barbarous dictatorships known in history, with the rise of Hitler in Germany. There seemed to be no hope anywhere except by a complete break with capitalism.

As Anthony Crosland, a leading Labour right winger, wrote in 1956 about the atmosphere in his youth:

> The pervasive influence of Marxist analysis in the 1930s was a reflection of an intellectual ferment without parallel in the history of the British labour movement... More and more people came to feel that some thoroughgoing analysis was needed to explain the catastrophe which appeared to be engulfing world capitalism...

Things seemed very different a quarter of a century later. There was full employment in all the advanced industrial countries. Output seemed to be expanding inexorably with the longest boom the system had ever known. Real wages went up year after year, while even right wing governments provided welfare states to care for the poor, the sick and the old. Nazism seemed like a nightmare from long ago as parliamentary democracy stabilised in advanced countries and began to make inroads in the less developed South European countries.

This was the background against which many intellectuals who had once proclaimed their belief in Marxism now insisted it no longer applied. They accepted the then prevailing orthodoxy that crises were a thing of the past and that the class struggle was withering away. Capitalism, they insisted, was slowly changing into a post-capitalist 'affluent' society in which the only argument was over how exactly to spread the benefits of limitless wealth and ever greater leisure time.

Crosland put the argument in a highly influential book, *The Future of Socialism*:

> The belief that the 'inner contradictions' of capitalism would lead first to a gradual pauperisation of the masses and ultimately to the collapse of the whole system has by now been rather obviously disproved... Full employment has replaced depression, the instability

is vastly less, and the rate of growth appreciably more... The present rate of growth will continue, and the future is more likely to be characterised by inflation than by unemployment... Almost all the basic characteristic features of traditional pre-1914 capitalism have been either greatly modified or completely transformed.

This had occurred, he claimed, because the state had succeeded in taking the key economic decisions out of the hands of old style capitalists who were only interested in profits:

The capitalist business class has lost [its] commanding position... Decisive sources and levers of economic power have been transferred from private to other hands... Acting mainly through the budget, though with the aid of other instruments, the government can exert any influence it likes on income distribution and can also determine within broad limits the division of total output between consumption, investment, exports and social expenditure... The economic power of the capital market and the finance houses, and hence capitalist financial control over industry are much weaker. This change makes it absurd now to speak of a capitalist ruling class.

Such were the arguments which led the leadership of the British Labour Party to make their first concerted effort, in 1959, to ditch the party's 40 year old commitment to 'common ownership of the means of production, distribution and exchange'. Although the leadership eventually backed off from this change, their arguments did strike a chord with many workers, who no longer saw political action to challenge the system as a priority.

Twenty years later things had turned full circle again. The great post-war boom came to an end with the recession of 1974-76, and suddenly the Keynesian methods in which people like Crosland had put their faith no longer seemed to work.

Crosland himself now admitted his earlier account had been too glib, although he still tried to defend its essentials. 'Extreme class inequalities remain, poverty is far from eliminated, the economy is in a state of semi-permanent crisis and inflation is rampant', he wrote in 1974. 'British society— slow moving, rigid, class ridden, —has proven much harder to change than was supposed... The early revisionist writings were too complacent in tone...'

In the next two years, as the inability of Keynesian methods to deal with the recession became evident, literally hundreds of economists and economic journalists who had been convinced Keynesians suddenly switched to the 'monetarist' doctrines of the pre-1930s orthodoxy. Politicians were quick to join the rush. In Britain the Labour prime minister, James Callaghan, embraced the new doctrine in public at the 1976 party conference:

> We used to think you could just spend your way out of recession by cutting taxes and boosting government borrowing... That option no longer exists; and in so far as it ever did exist, it worked by injecting inflation into the economy. And each time that has happened, the average level of unemployment has risen.

His government's 'alternative' to Keynesianism was to allow unemployment to more than double while imposing an International Monetary Fund programme that cut £8 billion (equivalent to more than £20 billion today) off the welfare budget.

Even on Labour's right there were a few senior figures horrified at what was happening. Crosland, the man who had insisted in 1956 that Britain was no longer capitalist, now told stunned Foreign Office officials, 'The IMF is a capitalist body, it's intolerable that a socialist government should have its philosophy imposed on it'.

Yet people like Crosland found it impossible to shift the rest of the Labour government. The only alternative they could suggest to the IMF programme was to impose import controls, as governments right across the world had done in the 1930s. But their colleagues and their advisers insisted these would not work, and they ended up caving in to exactly the policies of unemployment and welfare cuts that Keynesians had once said would never again be necessary.

The experience of the British Labour government was not an isolated one. It was repeated in the 1980s in France, where the Mitterrand Socialist Party government abandoned Keynesian attempts at 'reflation' for policies that resulted in nearly four million unemployed; and in Sweden, where a Social Democrat government followed policies which left the archetypical Social Democrat dreamland suffering 14 percent unemployment.

The harsh reality was that Keynesianism did not work.

For a time in the early 1980s a last attempt was made to revive Keynesian policies in Britain by the left of the Labour Party. They elaborated an 'alternative economic strategy' which they entitled 'socialist'. In fact, it centred on the old belief of Keynes and

Crosland that a high degree of state control, including import controls, could lead the private capitalist section of the economy out of recession. In any case, by the late 1980s many of the best known proponents of the policy had abandoned it. Former leading left wingers like Robin Cook, David Blunkett and Clare Short were soon to endorse the new Clause Four with its espousal of the 'rigours of the market'.

21 Fatal flaws

The failure of 'Keynesian' state intervention to stop capitalist crisis in the West was matched by the Stalinist economies of the East sliding into crisis. This increased the confusion of those in the West and the 'third world' who had looked to the state to overcome the absurdities of capitalism. So long as the Eastern economies seemed to be going from strength to strength, their example was used to justify policies to build up investment and competitiveness through state controls in the West. If only Stalinism could somehow be combined with parliamentary democracy, much of the left claimed, then there was a way of getting out of the crisis through a programme of reform.

But such a view could not survive events in the 1980s when it became clear that the Eastern states were beginning to collapse economically. Poland went through a characteristic boom-slump cycle in the late 1970s and early 1980s—and, in the process, saw the rise of the mass workers' movement Solidarnosc and its crushing by military rule. From 1986 onwards the leader of the USSR, Mikhail Gorbachev, revealed its economy was suffering from 'stagnation'—until he himself fell from power as stagnation gave way to a slump as great as that in the West in the inter-war years.

As the Berlin Wall fell and the USSR disintegrated, many of those who had seen socialism as a mixture of Stalin and Keynes now claimed that capitalism had proved its superiority to socialism.

In reality, what failed was not socialism, but the strategy of overcoming the old crises of market capitalism through state capitalism. This left rulers and ruled alike helpless in the face of further crises—as was shown in the West with the deep recession which began in 1990 and in the East with the failure of privatisation and the market to bring the deepening slump to an end.

There had been a phase of capitalist history during which the methods of military state capitalism could ward off crises. But the phase had passed. Then nothing governments tried could put things right again.

This had been foreseen by the pioneering Marxist studies of military state capitalism made at the height of the post-war boom by people like Vance and Kidron. They had pointed out in the 1950s and 1960s that military state capitalism contained inbuilt flaws which were ignored by Keynesians and apologists for Stalinism alike.

First, competition between the great powers led them to undertake forms of military production that involved ever greater amounts of capital investment per worker. Typically, bomber production was increasingly supplanted by missile production, battleship production by nuclear submarine production. Plants like Boeing's in Seattle which had once employed 120,000 people would soon employ less than half that number. Consequently a level of arms spending that would provide full employment for the economy as a whole in the early 1950s would not be able to do so by the early 1970s.

Second, arms spending by the great powers provided a market for many smaller countries that did not themselves spend significantly on arms. So the US, spending more than 8 percent of its national product on arms, bought TVs, cars and steel produced from Japan which, spending less than 0.5 percent on arms, was able to devote massive resources to updating its civilian industries.

The industries of the low arms producing countries grew more quickly than those of their high arms competitors, and they came to make up a much bigger portion of the world system than they had two or three decades earlier. At the same time the high arms producers were under pressure to compete in civilian industries by diverting resources to them from arms: in the US the proportion of national output going into arms fell from about 12 percent in the early 1950s to around 7 percent in the 1970s.

But a decline in the overall proportion of the world system's investible resources going into arms production was to bring back to life all the old forces that create economic instability throughout the system. So the 1970s saw the first recessions since the 1930s affecting all the major Western economies at the same time. These years also saw the revival on a huge scale of the old tendencies pointed to by Marx—for investment throughout the system to rise much more quickly than the employed labour force and for the rate of profit to fall.

Finally, a third trend that had developed during the Great Boom fatally hampered the ability of national governments to cope with the crises.

The massive expansion of the system had been accompanied by a massive growth of world trade, at about twice the speed of world economic output. The sums flowing between banks in different countries on a typical day came to dwarf the foreign exchange deposits of national governments. This made it increasingly difficult for these governments to keep a check on what capitalists were doing with their funds. In the 1950s most governments assumed they could, for instance, establish a fixed exchange rate for their currencies; by the late 1980s many felt incapable of doing so.

The growth in trade was accompanied by an internationalisation of finance and production, as only firms that operated across national boundaries could afford to invest in the most advanced forms of technology. A handful of multinational giants came to dominate the aircraft industry, the computer and software industries, the motor industry, the telecommunications industry, the shipbuilding industry.

Capitalist governments which stopped their own national industries from collaborating with these firms risked losing access to the most modern techniques. But those that opted for collaboration handed control of key sections of industry to multinational capitalists whose concern was international profits, not national capitalist stability.

Governments found themselves increasingly powerless just as crises erupted on a scale not known for half a century. The British government in 1976-77 and the French government in 1981-82 were crippled by 'flights of currency' the moment they followed even the most minimal 'Keynesian methods'.

The political leaders of a host of 'third world' and 'newly industrialising' countries learned the same lesson the hard way in the course of the 1980s. As their economies began to show signs of crisis they rushed to embrace the market and 'structural adjustment programmes' provided by the IMF and the World Bank, in the futile hope that 'free market' capitalism would succeed where state capitalism was failing.

Things were not all that different in the Eastern states. They found their growth rates declining and their economies increasingly crippled by their attempts to compete from within narrow national boundaries with the larger Western economies. Even the biggest of the Eastern economies, the USSR, was less than half the size of the US economy whose arms production it tried to keep up with. When the US undertook a new round of arms spending with the 'second cold war' of the 1980s, the rulers of the USSR suddenly found they could cope no longer.

The only way out of this seemed to be to abandon the centrally directed military state capitalist economy for the free play of the uncontrolled world market, with its unpredictable ups and downs.

Hence the sudden 'discovery' by the rulers of all the Eastern bloc countries, from Hungary and Poland to China and Vietnam that 'socialism' did not work—a discovery which shattered the confidence of all the Western and 'third world' admirers of the old state capitalism. Hence too the remarkable spectacle of many life long socialists in the West and the 'third world' embracing the joys of the market economy in 1989-90, just as it was about to enter a new, devastating recession which proved how little, in essentials, it had changed since Marx tore its pretensions apart.

CHAPTER 5

Things fall apart

22 A new stage

C apitalism in the mid-1990s seems as different to capitalism in the mid-1950s as that did to capitalism in the early 1930s. Once more we are faced with high levels of joblessness, recurrent recessions, huge pools of poverty. Overproduction combines with cuts into welfare budgets and a downward pressure on wages that reduces still further the market for what is produced. Once again there is despair even among supporters of the existing system about its prospects. Will Hutton sums up a widespread mood when he writes of Britain:

> There is a mounting and quite proper sense of crisis spreading across all classes about the character and availability of work and its implications for every aspect of society—from the care of our children to the growing dereliction of our cities... Insecurity, low wages and wasted talent are widespread and the problem touches professions and occupations once thought inviolable.
>
> One in four of the country's males of working age is now unemployed or idle... The numbers living in poverty have grown to awesome proportions, and signs of social stress—from family breakdown to the growth of crime—mount almost daily... One in three children grows up in poverty...
>
> The country is increasingly divided against itself, with an arrogant officer class apparently indifferent to the other ranks it

85

commands. This privileged class is favoured with education, jobs, housing and pensions. At the other end of the scale more and more people discover that they are the new working poor, or live off the state in semi-poverty... In between there are growing numbers of people who are insecure, fearful for their jobs in an age of permanent 'downsizing', 'cost cutting' and 'casualisation' and ever more worried about their ability to maintain a decent standard of living.

Hutton tries to blame what is happening not on the tendencies of capitalism in general, but on the peculiarities of its British form, which he claims is distorted by the role of the financial institutions of the City of London. But he has to admit:

> What is happening in Britain is only a more acute version of what is happening elsewhere... There is scarcely a Western country that cannot tell us at least one tale similar to Britain... In the US job insecurity is endemic, and the wages of the bottom 10 percent of the labour force are about 25 percent lower than they are for the same group in Britain... Nearly one job in five in the US does not carry sufficient income to rear a family of four.

One of the most prominent theorists of 'the affluent society' of the 1950s and 1960s was J K Galbraith. His description of the US today is nearly as damning as Hutton's description of Britain:

> In 1988 the top 1 percent of family groupings had annual incomes that averaged $617,000 (about £8000 a week) and controlled 13.5 percent of all income before tax... The top 20 percent lived in some comfort with incomes of $50,000 a year (about £700 a week) and above. To them accrued 51.8 percent of all income before taxes... [Their] comfort and economic well being is being supported and enhanced by the presence in the modern economy of a large, highly useful, even essential class that does not share in the agreeable existence of the favoured community... [This class] is integrally a part of a larger economic process and serves the living standard and the comfort of the favoured community. The economically fortunate are heavily dependent on its presence... The poor in our economy are needed to do the work that the more fortunate do not do andwould find manifestly distasteful, even distressing.

Galbraith talks, confusingly, of a 'contented majority' of two thirds of people—but he means two thirds of those who bother to vote (half the electorate), not two thirds of the adult population. In fact, he notes, conditions for the great mass of the American population have been getting worse over the last decade and half, with four fifths of families seeing their incomes fall, with a fall for workers on the median wage of about 5 percent.

He also insists on the 'intrinsic tendency of capitalism to instability, to recession and depression', on 'the powerful tendency of the economic system to turn damagingly, not only on consumers, workers or the public at large, but ruthlessly inward on itself...' He writes of 'recession and depression made worse by long term economic desuetude, the danger implicit in autonomous military power, and growing unrest in the urban slums caused by worsening deprivation and hopelessness...'

He even makes a comparison between the US today and the USSR in the final years before it fell apart:

> Few things could have been further from accepted thought than the possibility that the explosive events in Eastern Europe could have a parallel in the United States or perhaps Britain. Communism had failed; capitalism was triumphant. Could anyone be so pessimistic to see that lurking in the successful system were grave flaws similarly concealed? Alas there are.

You do not, of course, get such damning indictments of what is happening from the economists of the Tory right. They are still trying to celebrate the collapse of the state run economies of the USSR and Eastern Europe. But even they have to accept that the system operates in a much more destructive way than was claimed in the 1950s or even the mid-1980s.

Former Tory chancellor Nigel Lawson can attack his successor, Clarke for failing to see the inevitability of the 'trade cycle' of boom and slump. The former enthusiast for monetarism, Samuel Brittan of the *Financial Times*, can note with puzzlement 'deep seated factors such as the trend away from "jobs for life" which is being experienced in all countries' and creating massive 'job insecurity'. Tory papers reflect the increasingly stressful life of those with jobs in headlines like 'Overwork: the middle class epidemic', even while they continue to push for still more overwork with calls to 'save on labour' and diatribes against 'old Spanish practices'. Meanwhile the 'new right' recognise in a back to front way the inability of the system to offer hope to many who live within it with calls for cutbacks in welfare benefits—even, in the case of Newt Gingrich in the US, extolling the 19th century work-house as a way of dealing with the 'underclass'.

Such a message is a far cry from that of the 1950s when even conservative politicians like Eisenhower in the US and Macmillan in Britain promised everyone a better life, when the American dream meant not merely success for those at the top but also security for those at the bottom, and when a British Tory government won an election around the slogans, 'We're all working class now' and 'You've never had it so good'. It is even a far cry from the 1980s, when Reagan in the US and Thatcher in Britain promised 'people's capitalism', with wealth 'trickling down' from the rich to the poor.

In their own ways, both the centre left and the right are recognising that the system has entered a new phase in the last quarter of the twentieth century—a phase remarkably similar, but on a much bigger scale, to that of the first quarter of the century.

The bare statistics show it. Rates of economic growth in all the advanced countries and in almost all the third world and the non-East Asian 'newly industrialising' countries have been lower since the mid-1970s than they were in the 25 years before.

Unemployment rates have risen, on average, over this period too. In the advanced countries levels of 8, 10 or even (in the case of Spain and Ireland) 20 percent are common. In the world as a whole, the United Nations estimates, there are a billion unemployed. Even in the most rapidly growing part of the world economy, the so called 'Chinese economic space' (China, Hong Kong, Taiwan, Singapore) growth is centred around certain areas, while in the vast Chinese hinterland hundreds of millions are desperate

Average rate of growth of real GDP per person employed

	1960-68	1979-88
US	2.6	0.9
Japan	8.8	3.1
W Germany	4.2	1.9
France	4.9	2.4
UK	2.7	2.6
Italy	6.3	1.6

to escape from rural poverty but cannot be provided with jobs in the cities.

The slowdown in growth rates reflects a fall in average profit rates, despite all the pressure to speed up work and hold pay down. Average profit rates in both the US and the European Union in the late 1980s were only about 60 percent of their level in the 1950s and 1960s.

Firms have responded to the pressure on profits as they always have in the past, with each trying to recoup its position by further cutbacks in the labour force and further 'capital intensive' investment.

The ratio of capital to labour has grown right cross the world. It grew by 2.4 percent a year in US 'productive industry' between 1977 and 1987; it rose by 2 percent a year for the British economy as a whole in the 1980s; it doubled in Chinese industry between 1985 and 1990; and in Latin America investment per worker grew by 2,000 dollars in the course of the 1980s. But this means new investment provides fewer and fewer new jobs. People are driven out of old, 'uncompetitive' sections of industry, without being provided with jobs in new, technologically advanced sectors.

Expansion of production using less and less labour could lead to a realisation of all of humanity's utopian dreams of the last 5,000 years—to a world without debilitating scarcity, to freedom from the pressure of work and to leisure for genuine creativity. But under the existing system it, instead, simply results in two devastating discrepancies. There is a growing imbalance between the level of investment and the level of profit required to sustain that investment. And there is a growing gap between the potential output of the economy and the ability of people's pay packets to provide 'effective demand'.

Productive capital accumulation takes place in fits and starts— suddenly surging forward and destroying old jobs, then, fearful of not making a profit, suddenly grinding to a halt and preventing the creation of new jobs. Firms slash workforces in order to keep ahead of their rivals and tell those workers who remain to toil ever harder. As competition grows ever more intense, firms devote ever greater resources to unproductive forms of competition—to expenditure on marketing and advertising, to promotion and packaging. And as average profit rates in industry fall, so there is an increasingly frenetic search for the profit to be gained

89

from speculation, in the world's stockmarkets, on office development and land values, in commodities markets, in foreign currencies. Trillions of dollars go into a whole world finance, of junk bonds and derivatives, apparently cut off from the real creation of wealth through work and machinery.

The system may have entered a new phase. But the way it operates is not new. It is, in its essentials, exactly the way described by Marx.

The only sense in which Marx is 'outdated' is not that the system is more rational than he thought, but rather his picture *understates* the destructiveness of the system. Capitalists do not merely battle against each other on markets. They also use the state to force rival capitalists to accept their dictates, supplementing economic competition with displays of military prowess. American capitalism seeks to persuade European and Japanese capitalism to accept its dictates by proving that it alone has the power to wage war in the vital oil rich regions of the Middle East; Iranian and Turkish capitalists rely on the help of their states as they compete with each other for influence and contracts in the southern belt of the former USSR; Turkish and Greek capitalists encourage a mini-arms race as each seeks to establish a dominant role in the Balkan countries once controlled by Russia; Germany backs Croatia, the US backs the Bosnian Muslims, and Greece backs the Serbs in horrific wars in former Yugoslavia; the Russian military wage vicious wars to hang on to vital oil pipelines through Chechnya and influence in the Tadjik republic bordering Afghanistan; China, the Philippines, Malaysia and Vietnam clash over control of the oil reserves thought to lie close to uninhabited islands in the China Sea; Israel tries to carve Egypt out from economic influence in the Arabian peninsular.

The result is that at any point in time there are half a dozen wars or civil wars, using the most horrendous forms of 'conventional' weaponry, in one part of the world or another.

Alongside the slaughter and devastation afflicting ever wider sections of humanity is another threat to us all which was hardly visible in Marx's time—the threat of destruction of the environment we depend on to survive. Marx and Engels were fully aware that the mad drive to capital accumulation led to pollution, the poisoning of the ground and the air, the adulteration of foodstuffs and the spread of horrific epidemics. Engels wrote vividly of these things in his book *Anti-Dühring*. But they lived in a time when capitalist industry was confined to relatively small areas of the globe and the devastation was local devastation, affecting chiefly the workers employed in a particular factory, mill or mining village. Today capitalist industry operates on a global scale and its impact is on the global environment—as is shown by the way in which the radioactive clouds from Chernobyl spread out across the whole of Europe, by the way in which the seas are being fished clean of fish, by the damage to the ozone layer by the gases used in aerosols and refrigerators. Above all there is the threat of the 'greenhouse' gases destabilising the whole world's climate, flooding low lying countries and turning fertile regions into deserts.

This is the state of affairs which defenders of the capitalist market expect us to glory in.

23 No more answers

The prospects look dire for the existing system—and for the five billion people who live under it. The most farsighted believers in reform of the system see this. 'Unless Western capitalism in general and British capitalism in particular can accept that they have responsibilities to the social and political world in which they are embedded', warns Will Hutton, 'they are headed for perdition.'

Yet attempts to reform the system are infinitely less successful than they seemed to be in the 1950s, or even in the 1890s.

Hutton himself notes that in Sweden, which used to be portrayed as the finest example of social democratic regulation of capitalism, 'the first attacks on the welfare state since the 1930s' came from a social democrat government 'curbing the rise in government borrowing', while in France the Socialist Party government of the late 1980s embraced 'competitive deflation and economic rigour', leading to 'youth unemployment even higher than in Britain'. 'Spanish Socialists and the New Zealand Labour Party' have been 'no less enthusiastic about budget cutting, privatisation and restructuring the welfare state than say the Canadian Conservatives. Everywhere the ideological edge of political competition has been blunted. Different political parties, when in government, offer similar programmes'.

In Britain, Labour economic spokesman Gordon Brown used a conference on 'global economic change' in 1994 to criticise past attempts at reform: 'Past Labour tried to counter the injustice and failure of free market force by substituting government for the market, and often saw tax, spend and borrow policies as the isolationist quick fix for national decline'. The *Independent on Sunday*—which goes along with many of Brown's ideas—summed up his speech with the headline, 'Brown ditches Keynes'.

Brown justified his stance by saying that the 'globalisation' of capitalism—that is the spread of multinational production and finance as well as marketing—rules out old style Keynesian attempts by national states to insulate themselves from the vagaries of the world economy. The argument has been more fully, and honestly, spelt out by one of Brown's former advisers. Professor Meghnad Desai of the London School of Economics, in a series of columns in the paper *Tribune*, argues:

> It is no longer possible to pursue left Keynesian policies in a single country context... We are now witnessing in the nineties a return to the sort of world socialists of the nineteenth century knew, with global movements of capital, and the state incapable of exercising much control over the economy...

'The lack of success of Socialist and Labour Party governments', he insists, does not result from 'a failure of will, or the pusillanimity of the leadership. The problem is the resurgence of capitalism... A century after Marx and Engels it continues constantly to reproduce itself.' This means even 'public ownership of the economy is no guarantee of control of the market...'

Such arguments have led the Labour leadership to jettison the old version of Clause Four of the party's constitution, with its commitment to 'common ownership of the means of production, distribution and exchange'. Their arguments, like those of the 'revisionist' thinkers of the 1890s and the 1950s, are that such formulations are 'out of date', ignoring 'fundamental changes' in capitalism. In this they are backed by would be 'left-of-centre' economists like Hutton and Desai.

Yet there is a vital difference between the arguments of the Labour Party leadership today and those used by the 'revisionists' Bernstein in the 1890s and Crosland in the 1950s. Bernstein and Crosland argued that the system did not require revolutionary or root and branch transformation since it was changing, on its own accord, into something rational and humane. Thus Bernstein insisted:

In all advanced countries we see the privileges of the capitalist bourgeoisie yielding step by step to democratic organisations… The common interest gains in power to an increasing extent as opposed to private interest and the elementary sway of economic forces ceases… Individuals and whole nations thus withdraw an ever greater part of their lives from the influence of necessity compelling them…

The increasing internationalisation of the system meant that giant crises were a thing of the past. 'The enormous extension of the world market has…increased the possibility of adjustment of disturbances… General commercial crises similar to the earlier ones are to be regarded as improbable'. Further, 'speculative momentum ceases to play a decisive role' in the major sectors of production.

Crosland, as we have seen, extended the argument, claiming government could 'exert any influence it likes on income distribution and determine within broad limits the division of total output between consumption, investment, exports and social expenditure'. This permitted it, he claimed, to guarantee full employment, to reduce the level of poverty, to increase workers' rights and to create conditions for 'equality'. It was this ability which made a socialist take over of the privately owned means of production 'unnecessary'.

By contrast, Blair, Brown and the others are saying the goal of social ownership has to be dropped because there is no way of stopping the domination of human beings by the economic compulsion of the market. The 'dynamism of the market and the rigours of competition' are welcomed in their rewrite of Clause Four—even though, as any Hayekite would point out, the 'dynamism of the market' is the 'creative destruction' of whole branches of industry and the livelihoods of those who work within them, while the 'rigours of competition' mean the pressure to work harder and longer for less.

The Labour leadership may not talk in such Hayekite terms themselves. But they accept the logic of the argument. They echo right wing politicians in saying people have to abandon the notion of 'jobs for life', they embrace the employers' demand for 'a flexible labour force', and they refuse to commit themselves to any promise of 'full employment'. Indeed, they have a worked out argument to the effect that past Labour governments appeared to fail because they promised things 'they could not deliver'. The only way to avoid this in future, they claim, is to promise virtually nothing. What they offer, in fact, is not Bernstein and Crosland's promise of unlimited reforms as the alternative to revolution, but a reformism without reforms.

24 Reformism's last fling

'Say what we mean and mean what we say' is a favourite sound-bite of the Labour Party leadership. But they can hardly admit in public that they can offer no reforms to the people who back them. So they juggle with particular arguments and rely on left of centre economists and journalists like Will Hutton and William Keegan to present them. These argue that there are alternative models of capitalism which work much better than that which has failed in Britain. The 'social market' and 'peoplist' (Hutton's term) forms that exist in Germany and Japan are held up as examples. Such models, it is claimed, give workers greater security so winning greater cooperation from them. This allows firms higher profits while at the same time offering workers a better deal. What is more, the subordination of finance capital to industrial capital in these countries makes it easier for them to escape from crises. The result, claims Hutton, is that in Germany:

> Unions forego the right to strike and to pursue their self-interests regardless of the firm's plight; but management eschews the right to run business autocratically in favour of the shareholders' narrow interests. Instead there is a compromise in favour of concerted and cooperative behaviour aimed at boosting production and investment... The German banks are stable backers of German industry and long term shareholders... This stability of ownership and financial support is matched by a welfare system which offers a high degree of social protection, the visible expression of social solidarity.
>
> East Asian and particularly Japanese capitalist structures emphasise trust, continuity, reputation and cooperation in economic relations... The firm is the core social unit of which individuals are members rather than simply workers... Income inequality is at the lower end of the international scale... The state seeks to build consensus and guides firms and the financial system in the direction established by the consensus.

The logic of both Hutton's and Keegan's (slightly different) arguments is for a reforming government in Britain to remodel British capitalism along these lines.

Yet it is not only the British model of capitalism that has been in crisis in the 1990s, but also the German and Japanese models. At the time of writing, Germany is emerging from a serious recession, with current levels of unemployment still above 8 percent in the west, up from the 2 percent of a quarter of a century ago. Real living standards of workers have been cut by a 'unity tax' designed to cover the costs of absorbing the east German economy into west German capitalism. The employers have provoked strikes in the key metal working industry in an unsuccessful attempt to hold wages down below the level of inflation and postpone the introduction of the 35 hour week. And there is a concerted campaign from an allegedly 'socially conscious' employing class to cut pensions and other welfare benefits.

As Hutton himself admits, his model is far from stable:

> Under the pressure of globalisation and intense cost competition the *Mittelstand* (medium sized firms) have begun to lose ground and there are fears that large German firms are being forced to get their supplies in low-cost countries while overseas producers are winning business in the *Mittelstand*'s heartlands. German banks, under the same pressures, are allegedly becoming more short term in their horizons... Large firms, determined to emulate the Japanese and contain costs by sub-contracting out work and insisting on 'just-in-time' delivery, are asking suppliers to become ever more flexible.

As for the 'far eastern' model, Hutton admits it has always involved 'long hours and often demeaning working conditions'. What is more it has usually been imposed by one party states (as are Taiwan, China, Singapore and as Japan effectively was for 40 years), or military dictatorships (Korea).

The biggest East Asian economy, in Japan, is now encountering many of the same problems as in Britain, the US and continental Europe. It ran into deep crisis in the early 1990s. The solvency of its great banks has been threatened. The *Financial Times* reports 'a steady shift of production offshore' until 'about a sixth of manufacturing production is overseas', while 'many Japanese industries are burdened by excess capacity at home and face growing challenges abroad'. In 1994 unemployment rose to its highest level for 40 years, with only 64 jobs available for every 100 job seekers. It is difficult to see why the faltering Japanese and German capitalisms should offer a model for weaker capitalisms like that of Britain.

Talk of the 'European' or 'East Asian' model of capitalism is often linked to an argument about the importance of 'human capital'—the skills embodied in highly educated labour. Gordon Brown, for instance, has asserted that this is the key to capitalist development today rather than the means of production. Further, Brown claims this makes the 'old arguments' about who owns industry irrelevant.

The way for British capitalism to overcome its weaknesses, he argues, is for it to step up 'investment in human capital' through a greater stress on training a skilled workforce. The result then can be higher living standards and better social services paid for by higher productivity, as the economy enters a virtuous circle of rising output —so called 'endogenous growth'.

The argument contains three elementary fallacies. First, even the most highly skilled labour today does not take place on its own, without advanced means of production. In fact, it is more dependent on them than before, which is why the ratio of investment to labour continues to grow right round the world.

Second, there is no reason why any one country should be able to corner the supply of skilled labour. Even industrially backward countries like India and China contain many millions of highly educated people—with all the skills required for highly sophisticated jobs like civil engineering, software engineering and so on, let alone less highly skilled jobs like computer input and word-processing. Only a very small percentage of the total population may have these skills, but the total population is large enough for this small percentage to offer international capitalism comparable amounts of skilled labour as are to be found in many advanced countries. Meanwhile, advances in communications technology are making it possible for skilled design and computer tasks to be done in less advanced countries for transmission back to the advanced centres of production.

Under these circumstances, capitalists will use the threat of moving, say, software engineering to somewhere like Bangalore in India as a lever to cut the wages and worsen the working conditions of a workforce in Britain. Nothing Brown or Hutton is prepared to suggest will stop them.

Thirdly, even if 'human capital' were central, this would not stop the overall drive in both the world system and its British sector towards deeper crises. The pressures would still be on employers to reduce the levels of employment. So, for instance, the new communications technology known as 'telematics' based on 'the convergence between telecommunications and computing', far from enlarging employment, is destroying more jobs than it creates, according to a study by Professor John Goddard of Newcastle University. And nothing stops the devastation caused by periodic 'overproduction', a devastation that will get worse over time because of downward pressures on the rate of profit.

Raising the level of skills in a national economy cannot ward off the tendencies of capitalism towards crisis noted not only by Marx in the mid-19th century, but also by Keynes in the interwar years. For, to use the jargon of the economists, the question of skills concerns the 'supply side' of an economy, not the 'demand side'—and so can do nothing about the 'overproduction' and unemployment which Keynesianism used to claim to be able to deal with. In dropping that claim today's reformists are admitting they have no answers to the central problems facing the mass of people today—growing unemployment, job insecurity internationally, increased workloads and the pressure to accept lower living standards.

Hutton admits how limited the options for the national state are:

Foreigners own a quarter of British shares, bonds and bank deposits. The capitals markets' veto is particularly strong, and any British government will be imprisoned by their demands for fiscal and monetary caution.

His conclusion, however, is not to see that under such circumstances Keynesian reformism is an unworkable fantasy, but instead to claim Keynesianism on a European scale can work where national Keynesianism cannot:

Britain has a particular interest in the construction of a more stable international order. But the country cannot act on its own—and this is where the European Union and its potential for organising concerted action becomes crucial. The countries of the EU together have the power to regulate financial markets and control capital flows, and to play a part in compelling the US and Japan to manage their relationship better as part of a world deal. They have the

97

potential to manage demand, boosting and reducing it when necessary, without having their policies blown off course by capital markets… If Europe wants to defend its idea of a welfare state…it will have to do so in a united fashion.

However, any close examination of what has been called 'Euro keynesian' reformism proves it is as hollow as 'human capital' reformism. It assumes that the different European capitalist powers can simply sink their differences and cooperate economically, when so far they have failed to cooperate to maintain their currency parities within the European Monetary Union, or even to coordinate their foreign polices to deal with a civil war just across the Union's borders in former Yugoslavia.

In fact, in each country of the Union, large national companies have close relations with the national state and exert pressure on it to protect their interests against other companies and other countries.

What is more, the internationalisation of the system means that even governments of the largest economies in the world, those of the US and Japan, are increasingly restricted in what they can do by the pressures of worldwide competition. A united capitalist Europe would find itself subject to the same pressures. The response of big business would be to step up its pressures on governments to attack workers' conditions. Thus a *Financial Times* supplement 'Can Europe Compete?' published early in 1994 claimed the alternatives were either 'greater competitiveness, labour market deregulation and radical reform of the public sector' or 'Eurosclerosis' which would make 'the European Union a backwater of the global economy'.

Finally, and most importantly, the Eurokeynesians ignore the fact that the long post-war boom was not a result of Keynesian methods. Keynes no more caused the long boom than waking up in the morning causes the sun to rise. Rather, he signalled something which was happening anyway, as governments turned to a massive level of military spending and, with it, to massive intervention in the economy. Indeed, his own prescriptions for keeping booms going were rarely used during 'the golden age'. Strangely enough, Hutton, one of the most enthusiastic of the latter day Keynesians, has recognised as much in one of his columns for the *Guardian*, pointing to 'the proof offered by Robin Matthews as long ago as 1968 that the amount of Keynesian pump-priming to manage demand in the…1950s and 1960s…was comparatively small' and could not have been responsible for the long period of economic expansion. Attempts were made to use Keynesian methods in all the advanced countries when this period came to an end in the mid-1970s—and were abandoned everywhere because they did not work.

People like Hutton are wishing for the moon when they claim that such policies can work, if used on a European scale, 20 years later.

No doubt it is because they are dimly aware of this that politicians like Blair and Brown—and their equivalents in France, Germany, Italy, Spain and Scandinavia—refuse to promise improvements in welfare benefits, unemployment levels or working conditions. But this leaves them with economic policies hardly distinguishable from their Tory opponents.

Hutton has on occasion been forced to recognise this, as when he criticised 'the leader of the Labour Party' in the *Guardian* for delivering a speech 'that could have been delivered by Eddie George, Governor of the Bank of England, or Michael Camdessus of the International Monetary Fund… This is a position straight from the new right revolution of the 1970s, whose intellectual authors include Milton Friedman and Friedrich Hayek.'

25 Socialism or barbarism

'A reprise in the early 21st century of the conditions in the early part of this century'. Such is the danger that confronts the world if we cannot deal with the present crisis, concludes Will Hutton in his book *The State We're In*. Those 'conditions' included two world wars, the rise of Nazism, the collapse of democracy across most of Europe, the victory of Stalinism, the death camps and the Gulag. If they were to be repeated in a few years time, there is no doubt it would be on a much more horrific scale. We would be facing fascist regimes armed with nuclear weapons, with devastation and death on a scale that even Hitler could not imagine. We would indeed be facing a future of barbarism, if not the final destruction of the whole of humanity.

Warnings of such a future are not to be treated lightly. Already the crisis of the 1990s has begun to unleash the same barbaric forces we saw in the 1930s. In one country after another political adventurers who support the existing system are making careers for themselves by trying to scapegoat ethnic or religious minorities. In Russia the Hitler admirer, racist and proponent of nuclear war Zhirinovsky got 24 percent of the vote in the November 1993 poll. In Bombay another Hitler admirer, Bal Thackerey, runs the state government, threatening to wage war against the Muslim minority. In Turkey the government and the military wage a war against the Kurdish fifth of the population, while the fascists try to incite Sunni Muslims to murder Alawi Muslims. In Rwanda the former dictator unleashed a horrific slaughter of Tutsis by Hutus, while in neighbouring Burundi there is the threat of a slaughter of Hutus by Tutsis.

All this horror has its origins in the failure of market capitalism to provide even minimally satisfactory lives for the mass of people. Instead it leaves a fifth of the world's population under nourished and most of the rest doubting whether they will be able to enjoy tomorrow the small comforts allowed to them today.

Both the out and out defenders of ruling class power and today's timid and cowed reformists tell us there is no alternative to this system. But if that is true, then there is no hope for humanity. Politics becomes merely about moving the deckchairs on the *Titanic* while making sure no one disturbs the rich and privileged as they dine at the captain's table.

But there is an alternative. The whole crazy system of alienated labour is a product of what we do. Human beings have the power to seize control of the ways of creating wealth and to subordinate them to our decisions, to our values. We do not have to leave them to the blind caprice of the market, to the mad rush of rival owners of wealth in their race to keep ahead of each other. The new technologies that are available today, far from making our lives worse, have the potential to make this control easier. Automated work processes could provide us with more leisure, with more time for creativity and more chance to deliberate on where the world is going. Computerisation could provide us with unparalleled information about the resources available to satisfy our needs and how to deploy them effectively.

But this alternative cannot come from working within the system, from accepting the insane logic of the market, of competitive accumulation, of working harder in order to force someone else to work harder or lose their job. The alternative can only come from fighting against the system and the disastrous effect its logic has on the lives of the mass of people.

The reformists say that such a fight cannot succeed because of the 'globalisation' of the system. Globalisation is another way of saying the system is increasingly dominated by a relatively few giant industrial and financial institutions, each of which reaches out from its national home base to dominate the lives of millions of people in scores of countries. The power of those who run these institutions is greater than ever before when it comes to forcing into line—or forcing out of office—governments which try to regulate their activities.

But this does not mean those of us who want a humane society need to fight these institutions and the system they make up less than in the past. Quite the opposite. It means we have to fight harder, in a more determined way. It means that they will take a ruthless revenge on us if we fight half-heartedly, rather than seeing the struggle as one to the finish. The British social reformist R H Tawney once pointed out, in one of his more radical moments, 'You can peel an onion layer by layer, you cannot skin a tiger claw by claw'. By their talk of 'globalisation' the present day reformists are recognising that the system is a tiger, not a placid vegetable just awaiting parliamentary trimming as suggested by Crosland and his ilk 40 years ago. But though they see it as a tiger, today's reformists' conclusion is to let the beast run free. This is not a sane conclusion for anyone who does not want to be eaten alive.

Globalisation does not rule out a serious fight against the system. For it cuts both ways. The giant corporations are only strong so long as the millions of workers they employ around the world put up with their activities. They can be paralysed the moment a serious fightback starts. The very integration of their international operations can increase their vulnerability to action by workers in any one of their national constituents. What is more, an awareness of the multinational character of their employer can make workers in scores of countries see more concretely than ever before the common interests they share, as they are subject to the same disciplines, preached at by the same managers, even forced to wear the same company logo and sing the same company song.

Finally, the globalisation of communications means that workers in one part of the world are much more aware than ever before of what workers elsewhere are doing. Any upsurge of revolt can suddenly inspire people continents away. This happened back in

1968 with the national liberation struggle in Vietnam and the 'May events' in France. It happened in 1980 with the sudden rise of Solidarnosc in Poland. It happened through the mid-1980s with the sudden revival of the anti-apartheid struggle in South Africa. It happened again in 1994 with the Chiapas revolt in Mexico. It will happen the next time any great workers' revolt occurs anywhere.

The international nature of the capitalist system prevents any national government, however radical and however great its support from the mass of the people, from breaking completely with the pressures that emanate from the system. This is not, however, a new phenomenon. Marx and Engels stressed the international character of the struggle against capitalism a century and a half ago. The *Communist Manifesto* insisted that 'the workers have no fatherland' and ended, 'Workers of the world unite'. Eighty years ago, at the time of the First World War, the leaders of the workers' revolution in Russia established a 'Communist International' as the forerunner of the 'Communist United States of the World', precisely because they recognised that no single country, least of all one as backward as Russia was at the time, could create a society of plenty by cutting itself off from the resources and the technical advance existing outside its borders. Seventy years ago Leon Trotsky repeated this argument against Stalin, insisting that talk of 'socialism in one country' was a 'reactionary utopia', since the attempt to rebuild society in its entirety without access to the wealth existing within the whole world system of capitalism would inevitably fail.

But these arguments have never meant waiting for revolution to break out everywhere simultaneously. Every process has to start somewhere, and the process of confronting the alienation, the misery and the barbarism of capitalism is no exception. It can begin in any place that capitalism exists—and today that is virtually anywhere in the world. But it cannot achieve final success simply in one place. The very survival of a revolt that challenges the system—particularly in a country like Britain which has depended on imports of food, raw material and many other goods for at least two centuries—is dependent upon gaining the support of those who are inspired by the revolt outside its borders. Long term success in remoulding society depends on the spreading of the revolt. A single country that overthrows capitalism cannot survive on its own. But it can be the bridgehead which encourages successful revolt in much wider parts of the world system.

Opponents of socialism say that even with such a spread of socialism across wide areas of the world, attempts to escape from the dictates of the market are doomed to fail. Trying to organise every area of production so as to satisfy a million and one human needs, they claim, is an enterprise beyond anyone's abilities. All that can happen, they prophesy, is that a new ruling elite will emerge which will dictate to everyone else where they work and what they consume.

However, when Marx and Engels, Lenin and Trotsky talked about the transition to socialism they did not do so in terms of the state taking over all economic decision making overnight. What they stressed was that those who created the wealth had, through their democratic organisations, to take charge of the key decisions, the decisions that set the parameters within which the rest of the economy operated. The day after the socialist revolution, as the day before, the great mass of people would go to work in factories and offices, and would be paid in money for what they did. They would continue to spend this money as they wished to satisfy their consumption needs. What would change, however, was the representatives of 'the associated producers'—the delegates from the factories, offices, housing estates, pensioners groups and so on would decide on the overriding economic priorities. In particular, the major items of social investment would no longer be determined on the basis of blind competition between rival firms, but by cooperative decision making.

They recognised that every great change in history from one way of producing human livelihood to another has always involved both gradual (evolution) and sudden change (revolution). Thus the transition from feudalism to capitalism involved slow economic evolution over several centuries, as capitalist production for the market replaced feudal production in the more or less self contained manorial village, but also sudden, revolutionary political changes as the rising capitalist class ousted the old feudal ruling class from decisive positions of power. The point was that without the revolutionary change, the evolutionary change would have come to an abrupt halt and society would have started going backward rather than forward—as, in fact, it did when economic evolution was not accompanied by political revolution first of all through Europe in the 14th century and then in central

Europe in the 17th century.

In the same way, the replacement of capitalism by a new economic mechanism based on human cooperation cannot take place all at once overnight. It will, in fact, take many decades for people to learn to control consciously very many of the mass of productive processes that take place in a modern society, and in the interim they will have little choice but to continue to put up with the old market mechanisms. But by seizing political control and by taking over the major industries, they can begin making the central decisions, which would then exert an enormous influence on everything else which happened. They could, for instance, stop rival firms wasting enormous resources on setting up industrial facilities in competition with each other and then telling each other's workers they have to accept lower wages and harder work in order to pay for them. They could end the enormous waste on advertising, or on sending identical products in opposite directions around the world. They could turn the luxury homes of the rich into facilities which are so desperately needed by those made poor today. Overall they can begin to replace anarchy by conscious human decision.

When they do so, most of the decisions they have to take will be no more difficult than those taken by the handful of directors who dominate each major industry today. In Britain, for instance, four fifths of the processing and distribution of food is in the hands of five firms. Each of these firms has to coordinate, in a planned way, the production and distribution of thousands of items, trying to fit them in with the tastes of 50 million different men, women and children. They are able to do so, not because these directors are geniuses—in fact, many of them are typical upper class twits—but because their wealth enables them to employ large numbers of people with skills, using the most modern technology. But a huge portion of this skilled effort is wasted. The people with the skills are subject to competition between the rival firms and so are unable to cooperate with each other, with the people who work in food production and with those who consume the food. Instead, a huge amount of effort goes into aiding in the exploitation of the firms' workers on the one hand and moulding the tastes of the consumers in unhealthy ways on the other. The ownership and control of these major firms by a democratic workers' state, which based itself on the pooling of initiative from below in a cooperative manner, would actually make the coordination of production both simpler (since there would no longer be systematic duplication of efforts in rival firms) and more responsive to the real needs of the consumers.

That does not mean that such a socialist organisation of the major areas of production would be flawless. No doubt mistakes would be made, with overestimates of what people wanted in one sphere and underestimates in another sphere. No doubt there would be endless arguments about how exactly to proceed. No doubt there would be dissatisfaction as well as satisfaction. But these things would happen as passing incidents, not as something built into the very mechanism of the system. For at present no amount of argument on earth can correct the tendency to overproduction on the one hand and shortages of necessities on the other. The reason is that the system is not based on rational decisions made as a result of reasoned arguments between the mass of people, but on the efforts of small groups of rich people to subordinate everything to their competition with each other to get more riches.

It is this blind competition that is producing slumps and booms, growing unemployment alongside increased workloads, overproduction of goods and cutbacks in welfare provision, ever more horrific 'local' wars and bitter outbursts of ethnic and religious hatred.

Marx pointed out that whenever forms of class rule have clashed with changes in the way production was occurring two outcomes have been possible—the victory of a new class as a result of bitter struggles, or the throwing backwards of society through 'the mutual destruction of the contending classes'. The German-Polish revolutionary Rosa Luxemburg put the issue even more starkly. The choice under capitalism she said, was 'socialism or barbarism'.

If we look at the way society is developing today in many parts of the globe we can see, all too vividly, the face of barbarism. But we can also see struggles against the system that repeatedly throw up notions of real advance, based on solidarity, on cooperation, on people caring for each other as they consciously and collectively work out their own futures. Those who preach half-hearted reform of the existing system preach a capitulation to barbarism. Those of us who look to revolution see in these struggles the possibility of going forward, not back. There is still, as Marx and Engels wrote at the end of the *Communist Manifesto*, 'a world to win'.

Further reading

Chapter 1: A world gone mad

On Marxist economics

Karl Marx and Frederick Engels, *The Communist Manifesto* (International Publishers, 1995) is the best overall account of their views; Karl Marx, *Wage, Labour and Capital* (published together with *Wages, Price and Profit* by Bookmarks, 1996) is the easiest introduction to his account of exploitation; Isaac Ilyich Rubin, *History of Economic Thought* (Pluto Press, 1989) provides a very readable account of how Marx's ideas developed out of those of previous political economists like Adam Smith and Ricardo.

The criticism of marginalist economics

Paul Ormerod, *The Death of Economics* (Faber & Faber, 1995) contains a useful summary of the most recent academic attacks on orthodox economics; Chapter 4 of M Mitchell Waldrop, *Complexity* (Penguin, 1994) gives a journalistic account of orthodox economists discovering faults with their theories at a conference on chaos theory; Böhm-Bawerk and Hilferding, *Karl Marx and the Close of his System* (Orion, 1984) contains a classic debate between one of the founders of marginalist economics and one of the most influential Marxist economists of the first third of this century; Nikolai Bukharin, *The Economic Theory of the Leisure Classes*

(1915) is a further Marxist criticism of Böhm-Bawerk's approach.

On working hours
Juliet Schor, *The Overworked American*; B K Hunnicut, *Work Without End*.

On stress at work
C L Cooper and R Payne (eds), *Causes, Coping and Consequences of Stress at Work* (John Wiley, 1988); S G Wolf Jr and A J Firestone (eds), *Occupational Stress* (Littleton, 1986).

On pre-class societies
For a summary of some of the literature, see my 'Engels and the Origins of Human Society' in *International Socialism* 65 (Winter 1994).

On 'the primitive accumulation of capital'
One of the most readable sections of Marx's *Capital*, Volume 1 (Penguin, 1990), provides a harrowing account of the primitive accumulation of capital; Eric Williams, *Capitalism and Slavery* (University of North Carolina Press, 1994) deals with the importance of the slave trade to capitalist development.

Chapter 2: Explaining the crisis

The account of the most recent ups and downs of the capitalist system is spelt out at much greater length in a two part article I wrote in *International Socialism* 58 (Spring 1993) and 60 (Autumn 1993), 'Where is Capitalism Going?'. Most of my sources of empirical matter are referenced in this article.

On Hayek
C Nishiyama and K R Leube (eds), *The Essential Hayek*; Jim Tomlinson, *Hayek and the Market* (Pluto Press, 1990).

On Keynesianism
J M Keynes, *The General Theory of Employment* (Macmillan, 1963); Axel Leinjonhufvud, *On Keynesian Economics* (London, 1968); N G Mankiw and D Romer (eds), *New Keynesian Economics, Volume 1: Imperfect Competition and Sticky Prices* (MIT Press, 1991).

Chapter 3: Getting worse

The basic arguments of this section, together with sources and critical notes, are to be found in Chapter 1 of my book *Explaining the Crisis* (Bookmarks, 1984).

On Taylorism
Ed Andrew, *Closing the Iron Cage* (Black Rose Books, 1981); Harry Braverman, *Labour and Monopoly Capitalism* (Monthly Review Press, 1976).

On working hours
See sources for Chapter 1.

On the 19th century
E J Hobsbawm, *The Age of Empire* (Abacus, 1994), Chapter 2, 'An Economy Changes Gear'; M Flamant and J Singer-Kerel, *Modern Economic Crises* (London, 1970).

On the falling rate of profit
J Gillman, *The Falling Rate of Profit* (London, 1956); S Mage, *The 'law of the falling rate of profit', its place in the Marxian theoretical system and its relevance for the US economy* (PhD thesis, Columbia University, 1963); F Moseley, *The Falling Rate of Profit in the Post War United States Economy* (Macmillan, 1991).

On the capital-output ratio
Colin Clarke, *Oxford Economic Papers* (November 1978).

Chapter 4: Getting bigger

Once again the basic arguments of this section are to be found, with sources, in my book *Explaining the Crisis*—this time in Chapter 2, 'The Crisis Last Time', about the inter-war period.

On imperialism
N I Bukharin, *Imperialism and the World Economy* (Merlin Press, 1987); V I Lenin, *Imperialism, the Highest Stage of Capitalism* (International Publishers, 1993), E J Hobsbawm, *The Age of Empire*.

On militarism and state capitalism

Henryk Grossman, *The Law of Accumulation and Breakdown of the Capitalist System* (Pluto Press, 1992), pp157-8; H Draper (ed), *The Permanent Arms Economy* (Berkeley, 1970) contains reprints of some of Vance's writings; Mike Kidron, *The Permanent Arms Economy* (Socialist Workers Party, 1989) is a reprint of his seminal article from the first series of *International Socialism*); Mike Kidron, *Western Capitalism Since the War* (Penguin, 1968); Mike Kidron, *Capitalism and Theory* (Pluto Press, 1974).

On Stalinism

Tony Cliff, *State Capitalism in Russia* (Bookmarks, 1988); Chris Harman, *Class Struggles in Eastern Europe* (Bookmarks, 1988); Chris Harman, 'The Storm Breaks', *International Socialism* 46 (Spring 1990); Chris Harman, 'The State and Capitalism Today', *International Socialism* 51 (Summer 1991).

On 'revisionist' theories

Edward Bernstein, *Evolutionary Socialism* (London, 1909); Peter Gay, *The Dilemma of Democratic Socialism*; C A R Crosland, *The Future of Socialism* (London, 1956); Susan Crosland, *Anthony Crosland*.

Chapter 5: Things fall apart

For a more lengthy account of the 1980s and early 1990s, see my two part article, 'Where is Capitalism Going?' in *International Socialism* 58 and 60.

For Hutton's views, see Will Hutton, *The State We're In* (Jonathan Cape, 1994); for Galbraith's views on present day America, see J K Galbraith, *The Culture of Contentment* (Penguin, 1992); for Keegan's views, see William Keegan, *The Spectre of Capitalism* (Vintage, 1992); for Hobsbawm's views on the present, see E J Hobsbawm *The Age of Extremes* (Michael Joseph, 1994), chapters 14 ('The Crisis Decades') and 19 ('Towards the Millenium'); for a criticism of some of the problems with Hobsbawm's analysis, see the review by John Rees in *International Socialism* 66 (Spring 1995); for Meghnad Desai's views, see the transcript of a debate with myself in *Socialist Review* (June 1995).